McGRAW-HILL
SCIENCE

Macmillan/McGraw-Hill Edition

Richard Moyer • Lucy Daniel • Jay Hackett

H. Prentice Baptiste • Pamela Stryker • JoAnne Vasquez

NATIONAL
GEOGRAPHIC
SOCIETY

On the Cover:

The orange-spotted coral grouper is a hearty variety of reef fish that is native to the coral reefs of the Indian and Pacific Oceans. These and other varieties of grouper are often collected as young fry or fingerlings for aquaculture purposes. The young groupers are raised on fish farms to meet the increasing demand worldwide for fish as a food source.

Mc Graw Hill **Macmillan McGraw-Hill**

New York   Farmington

Program Authors

Dr. Lucy H. Daniel
Teacher, Consultant
Rutherford County Schools, North Carolina

Dr. Jay Hackett
Professor Emeritus of Earth Sciences
University of Northern Colorado

Dr. Richard H. Moyer
Professor of Science Education
University of Michigan-Dearborn

Dr. H. Prentice Baptiste
Professor of Science and Multicultural Education
New Mexico State University
Las Cruces, New Mexico

Pamela Stryker, M.Ed.
Elementary Educator and Science Consultant
Eanes Independent School District
Austin, Texas

Dr. JoAnne Vasquez
Elementary Science Education Consultant
Mesa Public Schools, Arizona
NSTA Past President

learning through listening

Students with print disabilities may be eligible to obtain an accessible, audio version of the pupil edition of this textbook. Please call Recording for the Blind & Dyslexic at 1-800-221-4792 for complete information.

NATIONAL
GEOGRAPHIC
SOCIETY
Washington, D.C.

The features in this textbook entitled "Invitation to Science," "Amazing Stories," and "People in Science," as well as the unit openers, were developed in collaboration with the National Geographic Society's School Publishing Division.

Macmillan/McGraw-Hill

A Division of The McGraw-Hill Companies

Published by Macmillan/McGraw-Hill, of McGraw-Hill Education, a division of The McGraw-Hill Companies, Inc., Two Penn Plaza, New York, New York 10121.

Printed in the United States of America

ISBN 0-02-280065-4 / 4

1 2 3 4 5 6 7 8 9 027 07 06 05 04 03 02

Life Science

Consultants

Dr. Carol Baskin
University of Kentucky
Lexington, KY

Dr. Joe W. Crim
University of Georgia
Athens, GA

Dr. Marie DiBerardino
Allegheny University of
Health Sciences
Philadelphia, PA

Dr. R. E. Duhrkopf
Baylor University
Waco, TX

Dr. Dennis L. Nelson
Montana State University
Bozeman, MT

Dr. Fred Sack
Ohio State University
Columbus, OH

Dr. Martin VanDyke
Denver, CO

Dr. E. Peter Volpe
Mercer University
Macon, GA

Earth Science

Consultants

Dr. Clarke Alexander
Skidaway Institute of
Oceanography
Savannah, GA

Dr. Suellen Cabe
Pembroke State University
Pembroke, NC

Dr. Thomas A. Davies
Texas A & M University
College Station, TX

Dr. Ed Geary
Geological Society of America
Boulder, CO

Dr. David C. Kopaska-Merkel
Geological Survey of Alabama
Tuscaloosa, AL

Physical Science

Consultants

Dr. Bonnie Buratti
Jet Propulsion Lab
Pasadena, CA

Dr. Shawn Carlson
Society of Amateur Scientists
San Diego, CA

Dr. Karen Kwitter
Williams College
Williamstown, MA

Dr. Steven Souza
Williamstown, MA

Dr. Joseph P. Straley
University of Kentucky
Lexington, KY

Dr. Thomas Troland
University of Kentucky
Lexington, KY

Dr. Josephine Davis Wallace
University of North Carolina
Charlotte, NC

Consultant for Primary Grades

Donna Harrell Lubcker
East Texas Baptist University
Marshall, TX

Teacher Panelists

Newark, NJ
First Avenue School
Jorge Alameda
Concetta Cioci
Neva Galasso
Bernadette Kazanjian-reviewer
Toby Marks
Janet Mayer-reviewer
Maria Tutela

Brooklyn, NY
P.S. 31
Janet Mantel
Paige McGlone
Madeline Pappas
Maria Puma-reviewer
P.S. 217
Rosemary Ahern
Charles Brown
Claudia Deeb-reviewer
Wendy Lerner
P.S. 225
Christine Calafiore
Annette Fisher-reviewer

P.S. 250
Melissa Kane
P.S. 277
Erica Cohen
Helena Conti
Anne Marie Corrado
Deborah Scott-DiClemente
Jeanne Fish
Diane Fromhartz
Tricia Hinz
Lisa Iside
Susan Malament
Joyce Menkes-reviewer
Elaine Noto
Jean Pennacchio
Jeffrey Hampton
Mwaka Yavana

Elmont, NY
Covert Avenue School
Arlene Connelly

Mt. Vernon, NY
Holmes School
Jennifer Cavallaro
Lou Ciofi
George DiFiore
Brenda Durante
Jennifer Hawkins-reviewer
Michelle Mazzotta
Catherine Moringiello
Mary Jane Oria-reviewer
Lucille Pierotti
Pia Vicario-reviewer

Ozone Park, NY
St. Elizabeth School
Joanne Cocchiola-reviewer
Helen DiPietra-reviewer
Barbara Kingston
Madeline Visco

St. Albans, NY
Orvia Williams

B
Animals as Living Things PAGE B1

| CHAPTER 3 Describing Animals | B2 |

Lesson 1 Animal Characteristics B4

   Process Skill Builder: **Observe** B10

   ☐ National Geographic STS:
   Helping Endangered Animals B12

Lesson 2 Animals Without Backbones B14

Lesson 3 Animals With Backbones B26

   ☐ National Geographic Amazing Stories:
   Spider Giants B38

Chapter Review B40

| CHAPTER 4 Life Processes | B42 |

Lesson 4 Organ Systems B44

Lesson 5 Development and Reproduction B54

Lesson 6 Animal Survival B64

   Process Skill Builder: **Form a Hypothesis** B69

   ☐ National Geographic Science Magazine:
   Dancing Bees B74

Chapter Review B76

   ☐ National Geographic People in Science/Careers B78

Unit Performance Assessment B80

For Your Reference

Science Handbook

Units of Measurement R2

Use a Hand Lens R4

Use a Microscope R5

Measure Time R6

Measure Length R7

Measure Mass R8

Measure Volume R9

Measure Weight/Force R10

Measure Temperature R11

Use Calculators R12

Use Computers R14

Make Graphs to Organize Data R16

Make Maps, Tables, Charts R18

Health Handbook

The Skeletal System R20

The Muscular System R23

The Circulatory System R24

The Respiratory System R26

Activity Pyramid/Food Guide Pyramid R27

The Digestive System R28

The Excretory System R29

The Nervous System R30

The Endocrine System R31

The Senses R32

The Immune System R34

Glossary

Glossary R35

Index

Index R53

Units of Measurement

Temperature

1. The temperature is 77 degrees Fahrenheit.

2. That is the same as 25 degrees Celsius.

3. Water boils at 212 degrees Fahrenheit.

4. Water freezes at 0 degrees Celsius.

Length and Area

1. This classroom is 10 meters wide and 20 meters long.

2. That means the area is 200 square meters.

2. 32 ounces is the same as 2 pounds.

3. The mass of the bat is 907 grams.

Mass and Weight

1. That baseball bat weighs 32 ounces.

Life Science

UNIT B

Animals as Living Things

NATIONAL GEOGRAPHIC

Animals as Living Things

CHAPTER 3

Describing Animals B2

CHAPTER 4

Life Processes B42

LOOK!

Young ostriches must grow a lot to become adults. Why do you think young ostriches stay close to their parent?

CHAPTER

3

LESSON 1

Animal
Characteristics, B4

LESSON 2

Animals Without
Backbones, B14

LESSON 3

Animals with
Backbones, B26

Describing Animals

Did You Ever Wonder?

Is there such a thing as a "free ride"? For these cattle egrets there is. The birds are riding on black rhinoceroses. They help the rhinos by cleaning the rhinos' backs of insects. This provides the birds with a source of food. In Africa these rhinos are endangered and many efforts are being made to protect them. What do animals need to survive?

Animal Characteristics

Get Ready

How would you describe animals? Think about any animals you know. Think about your pets or your friends' pets. Have you seen any animals in a zoo? Have you read any books about animals? Don't forget that you are an animal, too. What types of characteristics, or traits, do all animals have in common?

Process Skill

You infer when you form an idea from facts or observations.

Explore Activity

What Are Some Animal Characteristics?

Materials

clear container with aquarium water

water snail

goldfish or guppy

fish food

ruler

Procedure

BE CAREFUL! Handle animals with care.

1. Obtain a container with a fish and a snail in it.

2. **Observe** Record the shape and approximate size of both animals. Describe how each animal moves and any other observations that you make.

3. Add a few flakes of fish food to the beaker. What do the animals do? Record your observations.

4. What does the fish eat? The snail?

Drawing Conclusions

1. **Observe** What body parts does each animal have? How do they use these parts?

2. Compare how the fish and the snail move. Is movement an advantage for the animals?

3. **Infer** Do you think the fish and the snail are made of one cell or many cells? Why?

4. **Communicate** What are some characteristics that the fish and the snail have? Make a list. Compare your list with other groups' lists. Make a class list.

5. **Going Further: Infer** How are you similar to the fish and the snail? How are you different?

Main Idea Animals have many characteristics, including being able to move and to eat.

What Are Animals Like?

Here are some of the characteristics that all animals have in common.

Animals are made of many cells.

- Each cell has a nucleus and a cell membrane.
- Animal cells do not have a cell wall or chlorophyll, like plants.
- Different cells have different jobs. Bone cells support and protect. Nerve cells carry messages.

Animals reproduce.

- Some animals have thousands of offspring, or young, in their lifetimes. Others have only a few.
- Many animals care for and protect their offspring.

Animals move in some way.

- Most animals move during some time of their life.
- Animals move by walking, running, flying, gliding, crawling, and swimming.
- Animals move to find food, escape danger, find mates, and find a new home.

Animals grow and change.

- Some animals change form as they grow.
- Some animals just grow larger.

Animals eat food.

- Animals cannot make their own food, as plants do.
- They get food by eating plants or other animals.
- Animals digest food for energy.
- Animals use oxygen to turn their food into energy.

Some animals change form as they grow older. A caterpillar is an early stage in the life of a moth.

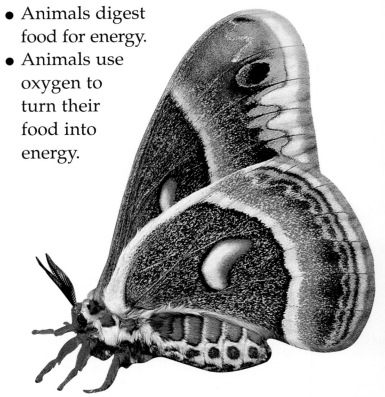

All living things need energy to stay alive. Animals get energy from food. A food chain shows how energy flows among a group of organisms. An ecosystem can have many different food chains. Combined, they form a food web. A food web shows how food chains in an ecosystem are related.

READING Outline
What do all animals have in common?

A Food Chain

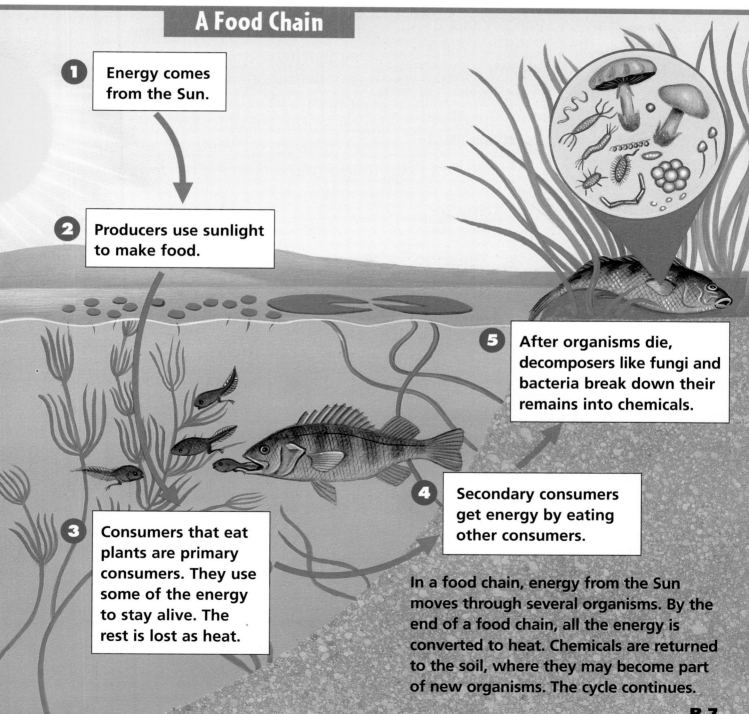

1 Energy comes from the Sun.

2 Producers use sunlight to make food.

3 Consumers that eat plants are primary consumers. They use some of the energy to stay alive. The rest is lost as heat.

4 Secondary consumers get energy by eating other consumers.

5 After organisms die, decomposers like fungi and bacteria break down their remains into chemicals.

In a food chain, energy from the Sun moves through several organisms. By the end of a food chain, all the energy is converted to heat. Chemicals are returned to the soil, where they may become part of new organisms. The cycle continues.

B 7

How Are Animals Different?

All animals have many characteristics in common. They are made of cells, they reproduce, they move in some way, they grow and change, and they eat food.

However, animals are also different in many ways. One major difference is having or not having a backbone. An animal with a backbone is called a **vertebrate** (VUR·tuh·brayt). An animal without a backbone is called an **invertebrate** (in·VUR·tuh·brit). You will learn more about vertebrates and invertebrates later in this chapter.

Symmetry

Another difference among animals is the way their body parts match up around a point or central line. This is known as **symmetry** (SIM·uh·tree). To study symmetry, fold a picture of an animal to match body parts. Body parts with symmetry match up as mirror images when they are folded over.

Some animals have no symmetry. One example is a sponge, the simplest kind of invertebrate. No matter how you might fold a sponge, its body parts do not match up.

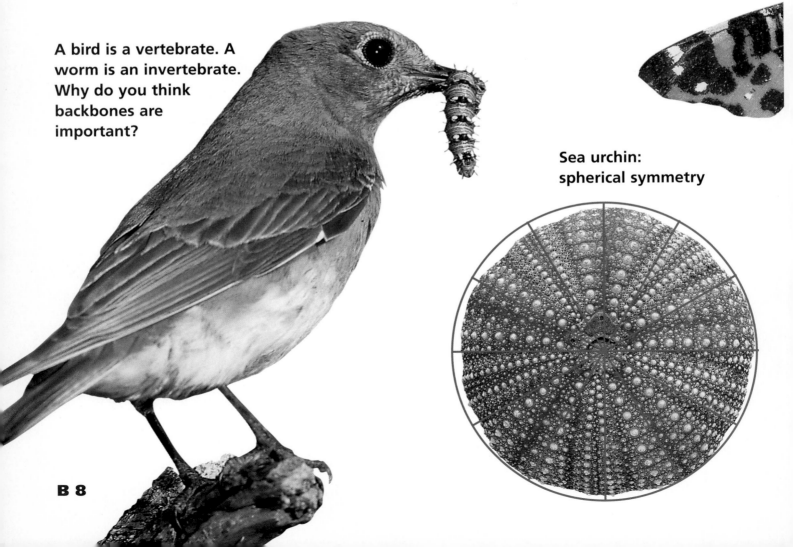

A bird is a vertebrate. A worm is an invertebrate. Why do you think backbones are important?

Sea urchin: spherical symmetry

An animal with *radial* (RAY·dee·uhl) symmetry has body parts that extend outward from a central point. You could fold a sea star through its center five ways and it would match up.

An animal with a sphere-shaped body, like a sea urchin, has *spherical* (SFER·i·kuhl) symmetry. You could fold a sea urchin any way through its center and it would match up.

An animal with *bilateral* (BIGH·LAT·uhr·uhl) symmetry has only two sides that are mirror images. You could fold a butterfly only one way through its center to have it match up. Organisms with bilateral symmetry have a definite front end, back end, upper side, and lower side. Vertebrates and some invertebrates have bilateral symmetry.

▶ **How are these animals different?**

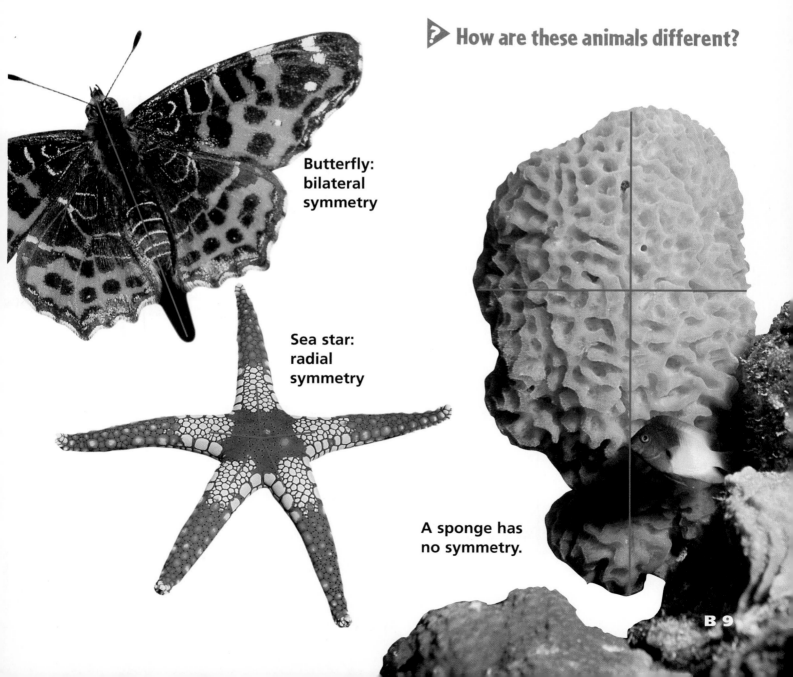

Butterfly: bilateral symmetry

Sea star: radial symmetry

A sponge has no symmetry.

Process Skill BUILDER

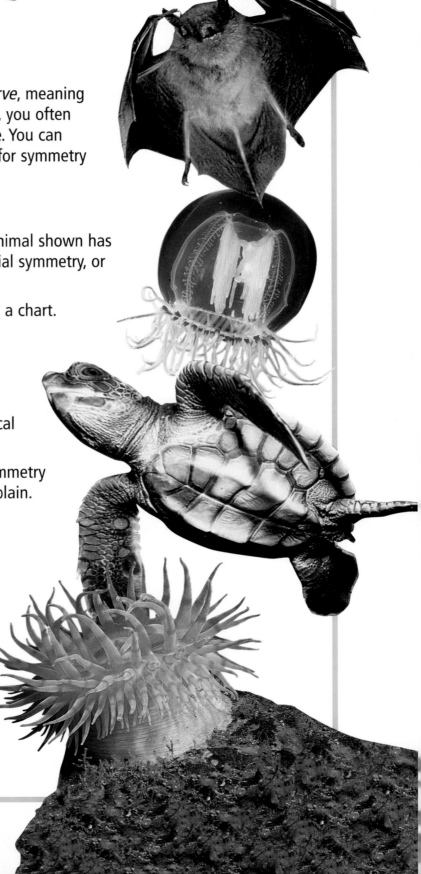

Animal Symmetry

A scientist's most important job is to *observe*, meaning to look closely. When you observe carefully, you often see things that you didn't know were there. You can practice your observation skills by looking for symmetry in different animals.

Procedure

1 Observe Determine whether each animal shown has no symmetry, spherical symmetry, radial symmetry, or bilateral symmetry.

2 Classify Record your observations in a chart.

Drawing Conclusions

1 Which animal or animals have radial symmetry? Bilateral symmetry?

2 Which animal or animals have spherical symmetry? No symmetry?

3 Infer Does an animal with radial symmetry have a front end and a back end? Explain.

Why It Matters

Identifying an animal isn't always an easy task. The organism to the right looks like a cross between a horse and a salad! In fact, it's a fish. Its wavy spines and leaflike appearance help conceal it on the seabed where it feeds. How might the fish's appearance help it survive?

Think and Write

1. What characteristics do all animals have?

2. What is the difference between a vertebrate and an invertebrate?

3. Compare radial symmetry and bilateral symmetry.

4. **Observe** What do you observe about yourself that shows you are an animal?

5. **Critical Thinking** What do you think would happen if one organism was removed from a food chain?

L·I·N·K·S

ART LINK

Draw a picture. What if you discovered a new organism? Draw a picture of this organism. Label the features you think are important for identifying it.

WRITING LINK

Write a paragraph. Is there anything unusual about your newly discovered organism? Describe where it lives, how it moves, and what it eats.

MATH LINK

Draw a diagram. What kind of symmetry does your own body have? Draw a diagram that shows how you could fold your body so each half matched up.

LITERATURE LINK

Read *The Polar Bear and the Jaguar* to learn about two animals who live in very different homes. Then try the activities at the end of the book.

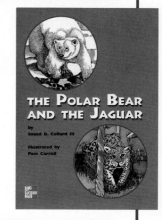

THE POLAR BEAR AND THE JAGUAR
by
Sneed B. Collard III
Illustrated by
Pam Carroll

TECHNOLOGY LINK

At the Computer Visit **www.mhscience02.com** for more links.

HELPING ENDANGERED ANIMALS

What are those creatures gliding through the water? They're manatees. These mammals spend their days slowly munching grasses in the water. That's why manatees are also called "sea cows"!

Unfortunately, people hunted the manatee. Its tough hide was used for making shoes and leather shields. Oil from its body was burned in lamps. Its bones had many uses, and the animal could

In the United States, most manatees live in the waters off Florida. Manatees are endangered. Trash in the water can choke and kill them. Fishing nets trap them. Boat propellers scar or kill them.

Many manatees are identified by their scars. Some are equipped with radio transmitters so that researchers can track them. When researchers find sick or injured manatees, they nurse them back to

The California condor is one of the largest flying birds in the world. It has a wingspan of about 2.5–3.1 meters (8–10 feet). Once thousands of these graceful giants soared over the wilds of the American West. Now much of that territory has been developed. Hunting and poisoning by pesticides also pushed the condor close to extinction.

Sadly there are only about 150 California condors alive, most of which are in captivity. In the early 1980s, scientists began capturing condors to protect them from extinction. Condors have been born under the watchful eye of scientists. A few have been released in the wild.

A falcon puppet is used to feed orphan birds.

Write ABOUT IT

1. What is killing manatees today?
2. Why would it be important to track manatees and condors?

AT THE COMPUTER
Visit www.mhscience02.com to learn more about endangered animals.

Animals Without Backbones

Vocabulary

cnidarian, B17

mollusk, B20

echinoderm, B20

endoskeleton, B20

arthropod, B21

exoskeleton, B21

Get Ready

How big are invertebrates? Some, like ants and earthworms, can fit in the palm of your hand. Others, like the octopus shown here, can grow much larger. Some are many meters wide! How else do you think invertebrates differ from one another?

Process Skills

You classify when you place things that share properties together in groups.

Explore Activity

What Are the Characteristics of Invertebrates?

Materials

living planarian

living earthworm

hand lens

petri dish

water

damp paper towel

toothpick

Procedure

BE CAREFUL! Be careful with live animals.

1 **Observe** Place the worm on the damp paper towel. Get a petri dish with a *planarian* (pluh·NAYR·ee·uhn) in it from your teacher. Observe each organism with a hand lens. Record your observations.

2 Gently touch the worm with your finger and the planarian with the toothpick. What do they do? Record your observations.

3 What characteristics of the praying mantis and magnified hydra do you observe? Record your observations.

Hydra

Praying mantis

Drawing Conclusions

1 **Define Based on Observations** What characteristics do you think invertebrates have? Make a list.

2 **Communicate** Compare your list with those of your classmates. Based on your observations, make a class list of invertebrate characteristics.

3 **Going Further: Classify** Think of other organisms that you would classify as invertebrates based on your observations. Make a list. Check your list as you continue this lesson.

What Are Invertebrates Like?

Invertebrates come in a variety of shapes and sizes. The one thing that they have in common is the one thing that they lack—a backbone.

Classifying Invertebrates

How many different types of animals do you think there are in the world? Would you believe more than one million? Keeping track of them must be a BIG JOB! The first step is to classify them into groups. Animals can be classified into two large groups—vertebrates and invertebrates.

Nearly 95 out of every 100 animals are invertebrates. Invertebrates are divided into smaller groups based on their characteristics. Each group is called a *phylum* (FIGH·luhm). You will learn about eight invertebrate phyla in this lesson. *Phyla* is the plural of *phylum*.

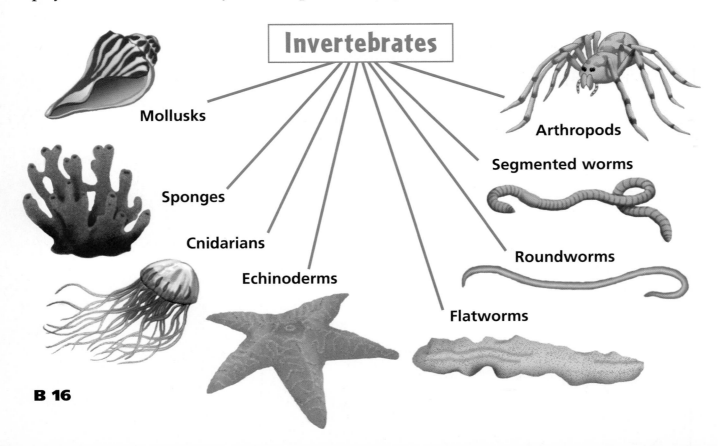

Invertebrates

Mollusks

Sponges

Cnidarians

Echinoderms

Arthropods

Segmented worms

Roundworms

Flatworms

A sea anemone's stingers don't hurt a clown fish. Slime on the clown fish's body protects it.

Sponges come in many shapes, sizes, and colors.

Sponges

Sponges are the simplest invertebrates. You've already seen a sponge on page B9. A sponge is shaped like a sack, with an opening at the top. Its body has no symmetry, is hollow, and does not have bones. It is made of two cell layers with a jellylike substance between the layers. A sponge can grow back a missing part.

Water flows into the sponge through holes in its body. The sponge filters the water for tiny scraps of food. Water and wastes move out through the opening at the top.

A young sponge moves until it finds a place to settle. An adult doesn't move from place to place.

Cnidarians

Imagine an animal that shoots poison darts at its enemies! **Cnidarians** (nigh·DAYR·ee·uhnz) are invertebrates that have poison stingers on tentacles. They use them to capture prey and for protection. Cnidarians, like sponges, have bodies that are two cell layers thick. Unlike sponges, they have simple tissues, a mouth, and radial symmetry.

There are three major cnidarian groups, or classes. The hydra is a member of one class. A hydra has a tube-shaped body and lives anchored to a surface. A jellyfish is a member of another class. It has a body shaped like an umbrella and floats freely in the water. Sea anemones and corals make up the third class. Groups of coral form coral reefs.

▷ **What are some simple invertebrates?**

How Are Worms Classified?

Flatworms

Worms are classified into several phyla. You will learn about three of these phyla.

A planarian is a type of flatworm. Flatworms are more complex than cnidarians or sponges, but they are the simplest worms. They have flat, ribbonlike bodies with a head and a tail. Their bodies have bilateral symmetry and are three cell layers thick.

One group of flatworms includes the planaria. Worms in this group live in fresh water and eat food with a mouth. Undigested food and wastes pass through the mouth, too. Another group includes parasites. They have no mouth or digestive system, and live and feed inside the bodies of other animals. They absorb digested food in the host's intestines.

An *Ascaris* can grow to 40 centimeters (16 inches) long. It can also lay up to 200,000 eggs a day!

Roundworms

Roundworms have a slender, rounded body with pointed ends. The *Ascaris* (AS·kuh·ruhs), hookworm, and vinegar eel are typical roundworms. Some roundworms, such as the *Ascaris* and hookworm, are parasites. They cause illness in people and other animals. About 2,500 species of roundworms are parasites of plants and animals. Others, such as the vinegar eel, do not depend on one particular organism for food or a place to live. They can live on land and in water.

Roundworms are more complex than flatworms. They have a one-way digestive system. In a one-way system, food comes into the body through one opening. Waste leaves through another opening at the opposite end of the animal's body.

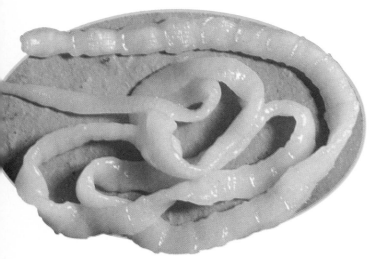

A tapeworm is a parasite that can live in many host animals, including people!

Segmented Worms

Have you ever seen or touched an earthworm? Earthworms, sandworms, and leeches are in the phylum of segmented worms.

Segmented worms have bodies that are divided into sections called segments. They have a three-layer body and bilateral symmetry. They have a digestive system with two openings. Food enters through the mouth. Wastes leave through an opening at the other end of the body.

The best-known segmented worm is the earthworm. An earthworm has a head end and a tail end. Every segment of its body, except for the first and last, has four pairs of tiny bristles. These bristles help the earthworm move through the soil.

An earthworm has complex organ systems that keep it alive. Blood is pumped through blood vessels by five pairs of simple hearts. Nerves give the worm information about its surroundings.

▷ **Why is an earthworm classified in a different group from a tapeworm?**

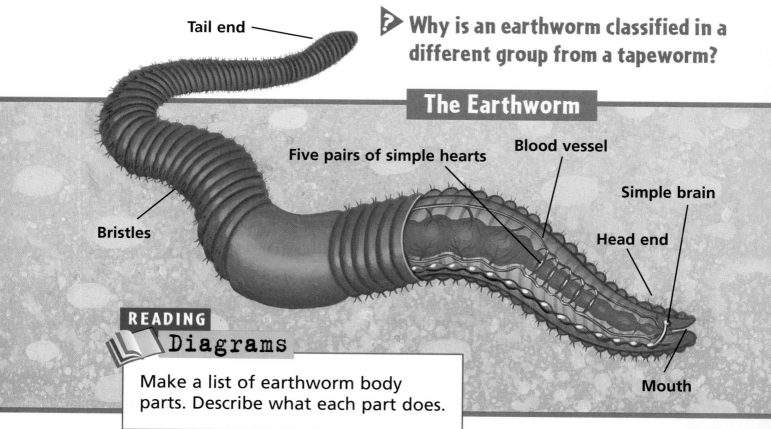

Tail end

The Earthworm

Five pairs of simple hearts

Blood vessel

Simple brain

Head end

Bristles

Mouth

READING
Diagrams

Make a list of earthworm body parts. Describe what each part does.

What Are Some Other Invertebrates?

Mollusks

Do you have a seashell collection? Most seashells come from **mollusks** (MAHL·uhsks). Mollusks are soft-bodied invertebrates. Some, such as snails and slugs, live on land. Others, such as clams, oysters, and squids, live in water. Most mollusks have bilateral symmetry and many organ systems.

Mollusks have many different kinds of shells. Snail-like mollusks have one shell. Clamlike mollusks have two shells. The group that includes octopuses and squids has lost its shell.

Echinoderms

Have you ever seen a sea star? It is an **echinoderm** (i·KIGH·nuh·durm). Echinoderms are spiny-skinned animals. You can identify most echinoderms by their star design and spiny skin. Echinoderms include sea stars, sand dollars, sea cucumbers, and sea urchins.

Echinoderms have an internal supporting structure called an **endoskeleton** (en·doh·SKEL·i·tuhn). Usually the endoskeleton has many protective spines. Many echinoderms move and grab things with tiny tube feet. Each tube foot is powered by suction.

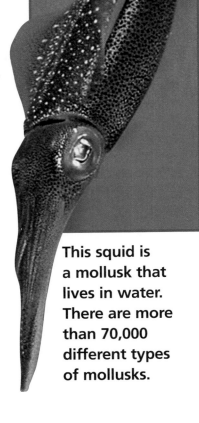

This squid is a mollusk that lives in water. There are more than 70,000 different types of mollusks.

The sea star uses its arms and tube feet to pry open the oyster. Then it turns its own stomach inside out. It sticks its stomach out to digest the oyster.

Arthropods

The largest invertebrate phylum is **arthropods** (AHR·thruh·pahdz). It is also the largest of all animal phyla. Arthropods live almost everywhere on Earth. Scientists think there are more than a million arthropod species!

Arthropods have jointed legs and a body that is divided into sections. Some arthropods breathe with gills. Others have an open-tube breathing system.

Arthropods have a hard skeleton on the outside of their bodies called an **exoskeleton** (ek·soh·SKEL·i·tuhn). It protects them and keeps them from drying out. Exoskeletons are made of a light but tough material called *chitin* (KIGH·tin). An exoskeleton does not grow, but is shed in a process called *molting*.

There are more arthropods than all other types of animals combined! You will learn about four main arthropod classes—arachnids (uh·RAK·nidz), centipedes and millipedes, crustaceans (krus·TAY·shuhnz), and insects.

▷ **What is the largest animal phylum?**

Scorpions feed on spiders and insects. Their sting can be dangerous to people and deadly to many small animals.

Arachnids

Include: Spiders, mites, scorpions, ticks, daddy-longlegs

Head: No antennae

Legs and Body: Four pairs of legs, two-section body, up to eight eyes

Home: A wide variety of habitats

Food: Most arachnids are hunters, mainly eating insects.

Special Features: Many arachnids are poisonous, including some spiders and scorpions. Some arachnids, such as spiders, can spin webs to trap their food.

Fact: Not all spiders are dangerous. Many are helpful to people. They eat insects and other pests.

What Are Some More Arthropod Groups?

Crustaceans

Include: Crabs, lobsters, shrimp, barnacles, crayfish, sow bugs

Head: Jawlike structures for crushing food and chewing; two pairs of antennae for sensing

Legs and Body: Ten or fewer legs, including claws. The body has sections.

Home: Some live in ocean or fresh water. A few live on land.

Food: Dead animal remains, seaweed, other leftovers

Special Features: Crabs and lobsters can have huge claws. One claw is often much bigger than the other. They use claws to fight and to scare off predators.

Facts: Many people enjoy eating shrimp, crabs, and lobsters. Crustaceans are also important foods for larger ocean animals.

Lobsters can live 50 years and grow to lengths of 60 centimeters (2 feet) or more.

Centipedes and Millipedes

Include: Centipedes, millipedes

Legs and Body: Centipedes: usually less than 100 legs. Millipedes: more than a hundred legs. Both have long, thin, segmented bodies.

Home: Under rocks, in rotting wood and other dark, damp places

Food: Centipedes eat worms, slugs, and insects. Millipedes eat plants.

How to Tell Them Apart: Centipedes have one pair of legs per segment and can move quickly. Millipedes have two pairs of legs per segment and move slowly.

Facts: Although *centi-* means "100," most centipedes have only 30 legs. Some have poison claws. A millipede's legs move in a wavelike motion.

Scolopendra (skah·luh·PEN·druh) centipedes can grow to a length of 30 centimeters (1 foot)!

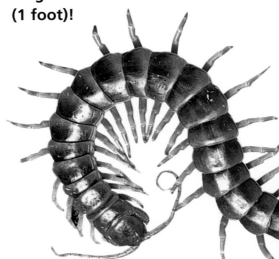

Insects

Include: Beetles, flies, bees, ants, mosquitoes, butterflies, dragonflies, fleas, termites, many others

Head: One pair of antennae

Legs and Body: Three pairs of legs; one or two pairs of wings; three body sections: head, thorax, abdomen

Home: Land, air, and fresh water

Food: Other animals and plants

Special Features: A special tube system for breathing; compound eyes made of hundreds of lenses

Facts: There are more different kinds of insects than there are all other kinds of animals. The first insects lived about 350 million years ago.

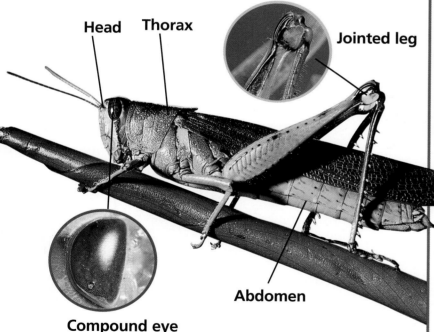

Head Thorax Jointed leg

Abdomen

Compound eye

READING Outline

What are three arthropod groups?

FOR SCHOOL OR HOME

Classifying Invertebrates

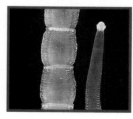
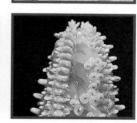

1. **Observe** Use clues in each picture to identify the type of invertebrate.

2. **Communicate** Make a table to show how you classified each picture. List key characteristics for each phylum.

3. How do you know the phylum that each animal belongs to?

B 23

What Invertebrates Live in Coral Reefs?

Imagine an animal that forms its own island! Corals do. Coral is made by colonies of polyps. Each polyp looks like a tiny sea anemone. For protection polyps build cup-shaped skeletons around their bodies. When polyps die, the skeletons remain. After many years they pile up. A coral reef or island forms.

Coral reefs contain invertebrates of almost every size and shape. A typical reef will have anemones, prawns, worms, lobsters, sea stars, jellyfish, and giant clams. Reefs also have more than 2,000 different kinds of fish—many with brilliant colors and unusual shapes. Coral reefs are among the richest communities on Earth.

Coral reefs are delicate. Coral needs warm, clean water to grow. Unfortunately, many coral reefs are threatened by pollution, souvenir hunters, ships, and boats. People take chunks of a coral reef as souvenirs. Ships crash into reefs. Small boats damage reefs with heavy anchors. It may take hundreds of years for the damaged reef to grow back.

What can we do to help protect coral reefs? We can stop pollution, boat carefully, not buy coral souvenirs, and learn more about reefs.

▷ **What types of invertebrates live in the Great Barrier Reef?**

The Great Barrier Reef, located near Australia, is about 2,000 kilometers (1,240 miles) long.

Why It Matters

Between 90 and 95 of every 100 animal species are invertebrates! Invertebrates are important because they are a food source for other animals. People also depend on them for many things. We eat clams, shrimp, and lobsters. Earthworms help enrich soil. This helps plants grow. Coral reefs protect islands and provide homes to animals. Water-absorbing sponges have many uses.

Even chitin is useful! Most people are not allergic to chitin. That is why it is often used to make contact lenses, artificial skin, and thread for stitches!

Think and Write

1. What is an invertebrate? How can you identify invertebrates?

2. How are segmented worms different from other worms?

3. What is an echinoderm? Give an example.

4. What threatens coral reefs? How can reefs be saved?

5. **Critical Thinking** How are all invertebrates alike? How are they different?

L·I·N·K·S

SOCIAL STUDIES LINK

Research a reef. Find the Great Barrier Reef on a map or a globe. Research what types of invertebrates make up the Great Barrier Reef.

ART LINK

Draw a picture. Draw a close-up picture of an invertebrate. Exchange pictures with a partner. Try to identify the animal and its phylum.

WRITING LINK

Write an expository paragraph. What if all invertebrates suddenly disappeared? How do you think this would affect life on Earth?

MATH LINK

Make a chart. Show the eight phyla of invertebrates. Give an example of an animal in each phylum.

TECHNOLOGY LINK

At the Computer Visit **www.mhscience02.com** for more links.

Animals with Backbones

Vocabulary

cold-blooded, B28

warm-blooded, B28

amphibian, B31

reptile, B32

mammal, B34

Get Ready

Did you know that you are classified into the same large group as fish, toads, snakes, birds, and rabbits? What could you all possibly have in common?

All these animals have a backbone. They are classified into a large group known as vertebrates. However, these animals are also very different from one another. These differences are used to make smaller groups.

Process Skill

You classify when you place things that share properties together in groups.

Explore Activity

What Are Vertebrates Like?

Procedure: Design Your Own

BE CAREFUL! Handle animals with care.

Observe As you observe each animal, look for answers to these questions. Record your observations. If you like, you can record sounds or take photographs to better observe these animals.

a. Where does it live—in water, on land, or both?

b. What color is it?

c. What kind of outer covering does it have?

d. What body parts does it have?

e. Do you see eyes, ears, nostrils, or other sense organs?

f. How does it move?

Drawing Conclusions

1 What major characteristics did you observe in each animal?

2 What are the main differences between a fish and a frog?

3 What are the major differences between a bird and a hamster?

4 **Going Further: Classify** Which animal in this activity are you most like? Why do you think so?

Main Idea Having a backbone gives animals many advantages.

What Are Vertebrates Like?

Although vertebrates have very different characteristics, they all have a backbone that is part of their endoskeleton.

An endoskeleton has two important jobs. First, it supports the body. It also protects the soft inner organs.

Classifying Vertebrates

The animal kingdom is divided into many invertebrate phyla and one chordate phylum. Vertebrates are part of the chordate phylum.

Vertebrates are divided into the seven classes shown below. They are also classified by how they control body temperature.

Fish, amphibians, and reptiles are **cold-blooded** . A cold-blooded animal gets heat from outside its body. Its body temperature changes with the temperature of its surroundings.

Birds and mammals are **warm-blooded** . Their body temperature doesn't change much. They use the energy from food to keep a constant body temperature.

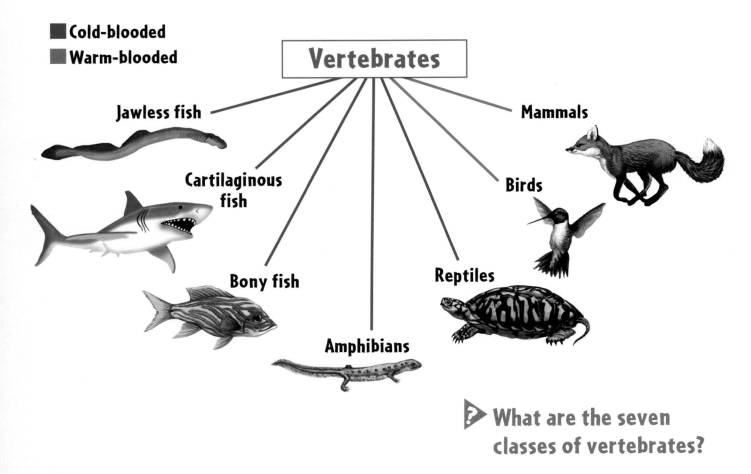

■ Cold-blooded
■ Warm-blooded

Vertebrates

Jawless fish

Cartilaginous fish

Bony fish

Amphibians

Reptiles

Birds

Mammals

▷ What are the seven classes of vertebrates?

What Do Fish Have in Common?

There are three classes of fish—jawless fish, *cartilaginous* (kahr·tuh·LAJ·uh·nuhs) *fish*, and bony fish. All fish have several characteristics.

- Fish are cold-blooded vertebrates that live in fresh or salt water.
- Fish have streamlined bodies and gills for breathing.
- Gills take oxygen out of water. They also get rid of carbon dioxide.

Jawless Fish

What do you notice about the eel-like animals shown here? They do not look much like other fish! These fish are jawless fish.

Jawless fish are soft and slimy. Instead of jaws they have powerful suckerlike mouths. A jawless fish uses its mouth to attach itself to another animal. It uses a horn tooth to cut a hole. Then it slowly sucks out the fluids and insides of the animal.

Jawless fish include lampreys and hagfish. These fish have no scales and unusual fins. Their bodies have a rubbery skeleton made of cartilage. Cartilage is a tough, flexible tissue. Your outer ears are made of cartilage.

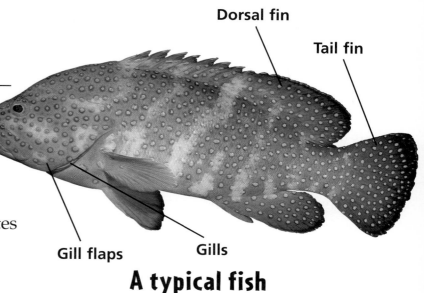

Dorsal fin

Tail fin

Gill flaps

Gills

A typical fish

▷ **In what ways are all fish alike?**

Lampreys are jawless fish. Most lampreys live in fresh water.

What Other Kinds of Fish Are There?

Cartilaginous Fish

The major characteristic of a cartilaginous fish is a skeleton made entirely of cartilage. Cartilaginous fish also have movable jaws, fins, and tough, sandpaper-like skin.

These fish include rays, skates, and sharks. Sharks are keen hunters. They can smell blood in the water from many meters away. With their razor-sharp teeth, sharks can tear apart prey in seconds. Most sharks, however, do not attack people. They feed on small fish and invertebrates.

Bony Fish

Have you ever gone fishing? If you ever caught a fish, it most likely was a fish from this class. Bony fish are the largest vertebrate class. They have jaws and skeletons made of bone. More than 21,000 different kinds of bony fish swim both in the ocean and in fresh water.

What makes bony fish so successful? Tough, overlapping scales protect their skin. Gill flaps protect their gills. Fins help the fish steer in the water.

Bony fish have different body plans. Predator fish have sleek bodies and powerful muscles. Reef fish have box-shaped bodies that fit in small spaces. Bottom dwellers are flat. Eels have snakelike shapes to fit into tight spaces.

The cichlid (SIK·lid) fish keeps its eggs in its mouth until the fish hatch. What type of advantage does this give the young fish?

▷ What is the largest vertebrate class?

Rays are bottom dwellers that eat invertebrates. This manta ray can grow to a length of more than 6 meters (20 feet).

What Do Amphibians Have in Common?

Have you ever seen a frog, toad, or salamander? If you have, how would you describe it? Frogs, toads, and salamanders are **amphibians** (am·FIB·ee·uhnz). An amphibian is a cold-blooded vertebrate that spends part of its life in water and part of its life on land.

Amphibians start out their lives in the water. A tadpole is a young frog. It has gills and fins. It cannot live on land because it has no lungs or legs. Over time the tadpole turns into a frog. It loses its gills and breathes through lungs and its skin. It also loses its fins and grows legs.

Although adult frogs live mostly on land, they are never far from water. An amphibian's skin will dry out without water. That is why amphibians live in wet or damp places.

▷ **What are three examples of amphibians?**

Frog

Toad

Salamanders are also amphibians.

What Do Reptiles Have in Common?

Do you think that a snake has a slimy skin? Some people think that **reptiles** (REP·tuhlz) such as snakes are slimy. In fact, reptile skin is dry. Reptiles have skin with scales or larger plates. Strong, waterproof skin helped reptiles become the first vertebrate group to live on land.

Reptiles are cold-blooded animals with a backbone and an endoskeleton. They have several traits that help them live on land. They breathe with lungs. Their skin keeps water from escaping out of their body. Their eggs are tougher than amphibian eggs. All of these traits helped reptiles become successful on land.

Reptiles can be classified into four smaller groups, called orders. There are four main reptile orders—tuataras (tew·uh·TAHR·uhz), turtles, lizards and snakes, and alligators and crocodiles.

▷ **Do reptiles have slimy skin?**

Reptiles	Interesting Facts
	**Tuataras** They're the smallest order. They're endangered. They live on islands off New Zealand.
	Turtles and tortoises Some tortoises can live more than 100 years! Sea turtles can swim up to 9 kilometers (6 miles) per hour.
	Lizards and snakes They are the biggest order. Lizards eat insects; snakes eat meat. Many snakes are not dangerous. Others are poisonous!
	Alligators and crocodiles They're the closest living relatives to dinosaurs. They can eat prey as big as a deer. They weigh up to 900 kilograms (1 ton)!

What Do Birds Have in Common?

Birds are vertebrates with several distinct characteristics. They have feathers. Feathers are light but very warm. They have beaks and no teeth. Birds have two legs with clawed feet. They have scales on their feet, like reptiles. Birds are warm-blooded like you. Unlike you, birds lay eggs with strong shells. Most birds sit on their eggs to keep them warm until they hatch. All birds have wings, and most birds can fly. Their bodies are designed for flight. Bird bones are light and thin. Bird lungs and flight muscles are powerful.

 **What is a bird?**

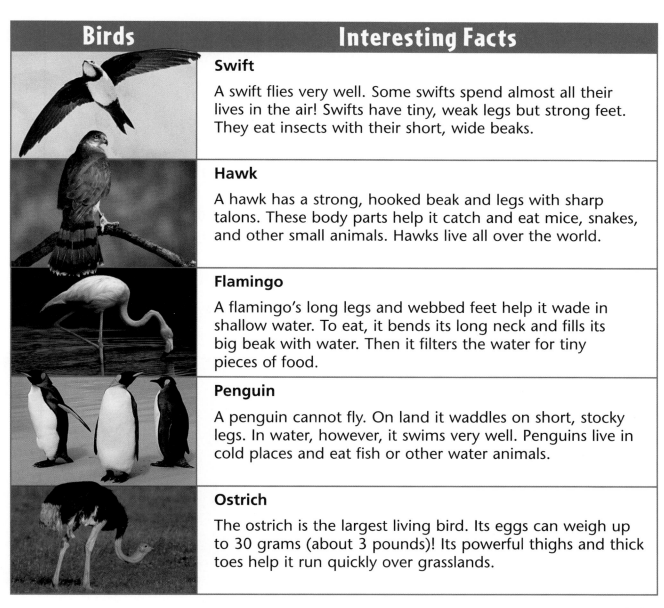

Birds	Interesting Facts
Swift	A swift flies very well. Some swifts spend almost all their lives in the air! Swifts have tiny, weak legs but strong feet. They eat insects with their short, wide beaks.
Hawk	A hawk has a strong, hooked beak and legs with sharp talons. These body parts help it catch and eat mice, snakes, and other small animals. Hawks live all over the world.
Flamingo	A flamingo's long legs and webbed feet help it wade in shallow water. To eat, it bends its long neck and fills its big beak with water. Then it filters the water for tiny pieces of food.
Penguin	A penguin cannot fly. On land it waddles on short, stocky legs. In water, however, it swims very well. Penguins live in cold places and eat fish or other water animals.
Ostrich	The ostrich is the largest living bird. Its eggs can weigh up to 30 grams (about 3 pounds)! Its powerful thighs and thick toes help it run quickly over grasslands.

What Do Mammals Have in Common?

Did you know that you are a **mammal** (MAM·uhl)? Mammals are the highest class of vertebrates. All mammals are warm-blooded and have hair. They can live in almost every kind of habitat. They can also learn! Female mammals produce milk to feed their young.

There are three basic groups of mammals.

Mammals That Lay Eggs

One group of mammals lays eggs. Only two members are alive today. They are the duckbilled platypus and the spiny anteater. Unlike most mammals, they have no teeth. The platypus has a muzzle like a duck's beak. The anteater has a tiny mouth with a sticky tongue.

A horse will rear on its back legs when startled. A horse kick can be deadly!

The cheetah is the fastest animal on land.

These platypus young hatched from eggs.

Although dolphins live underwater, they do not have gills. They come to the surface to breathe air.

Mammals with Pouches

Another group of mammals has pouches. It includes koalas, kangaroos, and opossums. These mammals stay in their mother's pouch until development is complete. Most live and graze on land. Some, like the koala in the photo, live in trees. Sugar gliders have a fold of skin under their arms that acts like a parachute, allowing them to glide in the air. Only one animal from this group, the water opossum, lives in water.

Mammals That Develop Inside

The largest group of mammals contains those that develop inside their mothers' bodies. These mammals include cats, horses, whales, bats, mice, apes, and humans—just to name a few! Rabbits are born after 30 days. Rhinoceroses are born after over a year!

After the young are born, they need to stay close to their female parent for milk. Adults also may protect the young from danger. As the young grow, they are better able to take care of themselves.

READING **Outline**
What are the characteristics of the three groups of mammals?

Classifying Vertebrates

1. **Classify** Use the clues in each picture to help you classify each animal.

2. **Communicate** Make a table to show how you classified each picture.

3. How do you know which class each animal belongs to?

How Can Animals Help People?

Sometimes people have a disability, get ill, or become sad. When people have troubles, animals can often help.

The photograph below shows Duffy. Duffy is part of a program called Pet Partners. Every week Duffy and other Pet Partners go to hospitals and other places. Their job is to help people who are sick, sad, or lonely to feel better.

Specially trained dogs often help a person who is blind. These dogs wear a harness with a handle. The person holds onto the handle and lets the dog guide them safely.

People who use a wheelchair often have trained dogs to help them, too. The dogs can help pull the wheelchair when the person gets tired. They can fetch things the person needs, such as glasses or a book. They also give lots of love.

Certain types of monkeys are also trained to help disabled people. They can act as a second pair of hands for someone who has trouble doing things without help.

Many animals are raised for food, clothing, or other products. Cows, sheep, and even goats give milk that people drink or make into cheeses. People use the wool from animals like sheep, llamas, and alpacas to make yarns. The yarns are used to knit blankets and sweaters, or are woven into fabrics. Certain animals are eaten for food by people who choose to eat meat.

Can you think of other ways animals can help people? Can you think of some ways people can help animals?

▷ **Why do you think it is important to respect animals?**

Duffy wears a special uniform. He has a blue harness and a special badge that says, "I am a visiting dog."

Why It Matters

Most invertebrates are small. Many vertebrates are very large, like the rhinoceros, the great white shark, and the polar bear. This is no coincidence. Backbones and endoskeletons give animals support. This support allows vertebrates to grow to very large sizes. You can learn much more about animals on the Internet. Visit **www.mhscience02.com** to do a research project on animals.

Think and Write

1. How are vertebrates different from invertebrates?

2. What is the difference between the three types of fish?

3. How can a Pet Partner help people?

4. Compare the three groups of mammals.

5. **Critical Thinking** A newt looks like a lizard, but it is an amphibian. What traits must a newt have?

L·I·N·K·S

LITERATURE LINK

Read *Penguins: Birds That Swim* to learn more about these fascinating creatures. Write about how they are different from most birds and how they are like them.

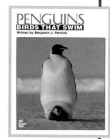

MATH LINK

Solve a problem. The humpback whale can weigh up to 36 metric tons (40 tons). How many pounds is that? Now find out how much you weigh. How many times heavier than you is the heaviest humpback whale?

SOCIAL STUDIES LINK

Do research. What animals live in your neighborhood? Pick a completely different kind of place, and research what kinds of animals live there. Compare the two groups of animals. Could an animal in your neighborhood live in the other neighborhood?

TECHNOLOGY LINK

At the Computer Visit **www.mhscience02.com** for more links.

Spider Giants

What's that creeping through the South American jungle? It's a Goliath birdeater spider, the world's biggest tarantula. It's big enough to cover a dinner plate! It eats not only birds, but lizards, mice, and other small animals.

A Goliath does not spin a web to catch its prey. Instead, it pounces on its victim and bites it with poisonous fangs. The poison kills the animal and softens its insides. The spider then sucks the juices out of the dead animal's body.

A Goliath uses its body hairs to sense movements nearby. The hairs also aid in defense. When attacked, a Goliath shoots out hairs from its stomach. The hairs can stick to an attacker and irritate its skin.

There are more than 800 different kinds of tarantulas in the world. Luckily, they're not all as big as the Goliath!

Close-up look at a Goliath's fangs

Write ABOUT IT

1. How does a Goliath spider kill its prey?
2. How does a Goliath spider defend itself?

This Goliath birdeater tarantula is from South America.

AT THE COMPUTER

Visit **www.mhscience02.com** to learn more about spiders and other animals of South America.

Vocabulary

Fill each blank with the best word or words from the list.

amphibian, B31   **mollusk,** B20

arthropod, B21   **reptile,** B32

cold-blooded, B28   **vertebrate,** B8

endoskeleton, B20   **warm-blooded,**
                        B28
exoskeleton, B21

invertebrate, B8

1. An animal that has a constant body temperature is called _____.

2. One example of a soft-bodied invertebrate is a(n) _____.

3. An animal with a backbone is called a(n) _____.

4. A cold-blooded vertebrate that lives on land and in water is a(n) _____.

5. The hard covering that protects an invertebrate's body is a(n) _____.

Use the words in the vocabulary list to describe these animals. Some words may be used more than once.

6. _____
7. _____
8. _____

9. _____
10. _____
11. _____

Test Prep

12. One reason mammals are different from reptiles is that mammals _____.

  A have a backbone

  B are warm-blooded

  C are cold-blooded

  D do not live in water

13. All birds are able to _____.

  F swim

  G fly

  H eat seeds

  J lay eggs

14. Which of these animals is a vertebrate?

   A octopus

   B snake

   C snail

   D coral

15. Which of these animals is an arthropod?

   F turtle

   G frog

   H sponge

   J ant

16. The body of a starfish has _____.

   A radial symmetry

   B spherical symmetry

   C bilateral symmetry

   D no symmetry

Concepts and Skills

17. Reading in Science Explain the difference between a food chain and a food web.

18. Product Ads The Happy Pet Company wants you to design a terrarium for iguanas. What would you put in the terrarium, and why?

19. Scientific Methods What if you discovered two animals that you had never seen before? They look very different but are similar in many ways. How could you tell if they were in the same phylum? Write down all the different ways you would compare and contrast them.

20. Critical Thinking All very large invertebrates, such as the octopus, live underwater. Explain why these large invertebrates could not live on land.

21. Process Skills: Observe Look at the pictures of the animals in this chapter. Make a chart that shows the classification of ten different animals. Choose animals from different phyla.

Boost *your test scores!*

Be Smart!
Visit www.mhscience02.com to learn more.

Life Processes

LESSON 4
Organ Systems, B44

LESSON 5
Development and Reproduction, B54

LESSON 6
Animal Survival, B64

Did You Ever Wonder?

Does the tomato frog actually eat tomatoes? No. It feasts primarily on invertebrates in the wild. In captivity it feeds mainly on crickets. Tomato frogs live in swampy areas of Madagascar. When tomato frogs are younger, they have yellow backs and dark legs. How do living things function?

Organ Systems

Vocabulary

circulatory
  system, B46

respiratory
  system, B47

excretory
  system, B47

digestive
  system, B49

nervous
  system, B50

skeletal system,
  B52

muscular
  system, B52

Get Ready

How do a fish and a frog compare? Think about their bodies and where they live. A frog breathes with lungs instead of gills. It has limbs instead of fins. It can live both on land and in water. Do you think a frog has organs and organ systems that are more complex than a fish's?

Process Skill

You **observe** when you use one or more senses to identify or learn about an object or event.

Explore Activity

How Does Blood Travel in Fish and Amphibian Hearts?

Materials

5 straws

two 7-oz cups, each with a hole in the bottom

three 3½-oz cups, each with a hole in the bottom

2 paper circles with flaps

5 labels

marking pen

tape

Procedure

1. Label each small cup "atrium." Label each large cup "ventricle."

2. **Make a Model: Fish Heart** Tape the paper circle with one flap over the top of one ventricle. Center the top of an atrium over the flap in the circle. Tape it to the paper.

3. Label one straw "From gills and body." Place it in the hole in the bottom of the atrium. Label another straw "To gills and body." Place it in the hole in the bottom of the ventricle. Draw the model.

4. **Make a Model: Amphibian Heart** Tape the paper circle with two flaps over the top of a ventricle. Center the top of an atrium over each flap. Tape the cups to the paper.

5. Label one straw "From body." Place it in the hole in the bottom of the right cup. Label another straw "From lungs." Place it in the hole in the bottom of the left cup. Label the third straw "To lungs and body." Place it in the hole in the paper between the two small cups. Draw the model.

Drawing Conclusions

Going Further: Observe How are the fish heart and the amphibian heart alike? Different?

Model fish heart

Model amphibian hea[rt]

Main Idea Animals have similar organ systems.

How Do Blood and Air Travel?

Blood is a liquid tissue. Blood carries food, oxygen, and water to the body's cells and removes wastes from cells.

The heart is the main organ that makes up the **circulatory system** (SUR·kyuh·luh·tawr·ee SIS·tuhm). Its job is to move blood through the body.

Sponges and cnidarians don't have a circulatory system. Materials move in and out of each thin body layer. Insects and other invertebrates have open circulatory systems. The heart bathes tissues in blood, which slowly drains back to the heart.

All vertebrates have a closed circulatory system. So do some invertebrates, such as earthworms. Blood travels through tubes called blood vessels.

A fish heart has two parts, or chambers. It allows blood carrying wastes and oxygen to mix. An amphibian heart has three chambers.

Mammals have hearts with four chambers, like the one shown below. They do not allow blood carrying waste gas, colored blue, to mix with blood carrying oxygen, colored red.

Aorta Ventricle Atrium Sinus venous

Fish Heart

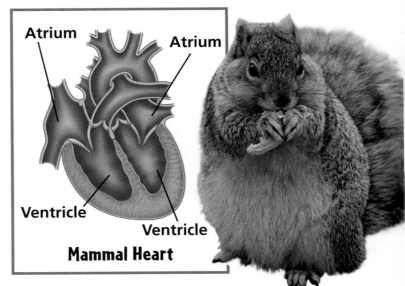

Atrium Atrium

Ventricle Ventricle

Mammal Heart

Circulatory System Facts

What: Heart, blood, blood vessels

Where: Throughout body

Jobs: Bring food, water, and oxygen to cells; remove waste

Who has it: All but sponges, cnidarians

Types: Open (many invertebrates), closed (vertebrates)

How Animals Get Oxygen

Cells need the oxygen carried by blood to get energy from food. The **respiratory system** (RES·puhr·uh·tawr·ee SIS·tuhm) brings oxygen to the blood and removes the waste gas carbon dioxide.

Most invertebrates don't have a specialized respiratory system at all. Their bodies usually are small. Gases can easily move in and out of tissues, even through their skin. An insect's exoskeleton has holes connected to tubes. These bring oxygen to different tissues.

Larger, more complex animals need a respiratory system. Each has one well designed for its body and where it lives. Fish and young amphibians have gills that exchange gases with the water. Adult amphibians breathe through both their skin and lungs.

How Liquid Wastes Leave the Body

Liquid wastes, created when cells break down chemicals, are removed by the **excretory system** (EK·skri·tawr·ee SIS·tuhm). Simple animals have simple systems. More complex animals, such as reptiles and humans, have two waste-removal organs called *kidneys* (KID·neez). They filter wastes from blood. The liquid waste is stored in the *bladder*, and then leaves the body.

Like many other small animals, earthworms take in air directly through their skin.

Respiratory System Facts

What: Lungs, gills, skin

Where: Open to outer air

Jobs: Bring oxygen into body, remove waste gases from body

Who has it: Vertebrates, large invertebrates, insects

Works with: The circulatory system to move gases in and out

—Air in

Lungs

In the human respiratory system, air travels between the mouth and lungs. In the lungs oxygen enters the blood and waste gas comes out.

▷ **What does blood do?**

Human Respiratory System

How Do Animals Take In and Digest Food?

Unlike plants, which make their own food, all animals must take in food for the energy they need to survive. The ways animals get food depend on their bodies and where they live.

An octopus and squid both have bodies made up of a head and tentacles. They use their tentacles to capture and kill the animals they eat.

A sea star has arms lined with tube feet. The tube feet provide powerful suction to move the sea star and pry open clam and mussel shells. The sea star then turns its stomach inside out between the open shells to break down and eat the animal inside.

Birds use their beaks to eat food. Some birds eat only seeds and fruits they pluck from trees and shrubs. Other birds eat meat. They use strong claws to catch and hold onto their food, which they tear into pieces with their beaks. Many meat-eating birds pluck fish out of the water, other birds from the air, or animals from the ground. Then they fly to a safe place to eat.

Lobsters and crabs have claws, too. Although they are different in shape from bird claws, they also are used to capture and hold foods.

Many frogs and lizards use long, sticky tongues to catch insects and other small animals. Many can move their tongues so fast you can hardly see it happen!

An osprey uses its strong claws to catch and hold onto a fish.

Claws help a crab capture a sea urchin.

Gotcha! The toad has used its sticky tongue to catch its next meal.

Frog's Digestive System

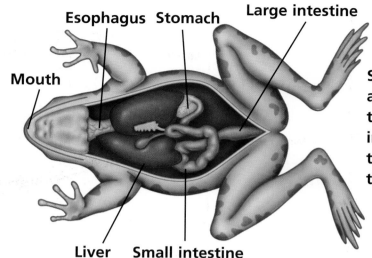

Food passes through the parts shown here. The stomach churns and mixes food. The liver adds chemicals to the small intestine, where food is broken down further and absorbed. Solid wastes pass through the large intestine and out of the body.

Mouth · **Esophagus** · **Stomach** · **Large intestine**

Solid wastes are passed to the large intestine, then out of the body.

Liver · **Small intestine**

Before body cells can use food for energy, it must be broken down. That is the job of the **digestive system** (di·JES·tiv SIS·tuhm).

In simple animals like sponges and cnidarians, cells along the body walls break down food into small particles. These cells transfer the particles to cells in the body.

Other simple invertebrates, like some flatworms, have a digestive system with one opening. Food enters through the mouth. Wastes and undigested food leave through the same opening.

A segmented worm has a digestive system with two openings. Food enters through the mouth. Wastes exit through the other end of the body.

Birds do not chew food. A muscular organ called a *gizzard* (GIZ·uhrd) stores pebbles that grind food before it enters the rest of the system.

A frog's digestive system is even more complex. Study the diagram. How does a frog take in and digest its food?

Digestive System Facts

What: Teeth, saliva, esophagus, stomach, intestines, liver, glands

Where: Hollow tube through body

Job: Break down food

How: Chewing, grinding, squeezing, chemicals

Types: One or two openings

Who has it: Vertebrates, most invertebrates

Works with: Circulatory system

READING **Main Idea and Supporting Details** What is the digestive system? What are some of its parts?

How Do Animals Sense Changes?

How do animals sense changes in their world and control their organ systems? The **nervous system** (NUR·vuhs SIS·tuhm) is the body's master control system. A nervous system is made of nerve cells joined to form nerves. More complex animals have a brain and some or all of the senses—sight, taste, hearing, touch, and smell.

Simple animals have simple nervous systems. More complicated animals have more complicated nervous systems. Vertebrates have the most complex nervous systems.

The structure of an animal's nervous system relates to its lifestyle. Compare the parts of the brain related to the senses of sight and smell in these three organisms.

Comparing Animal Brains

Shark Brain

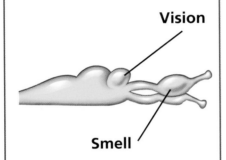

Vision

Smell

The shark has a keen sense of smell and poor eyesight. Brain parts related to smell are large in the shark brain.

Frog Brain

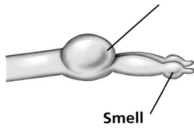

Vision

Smell

The frog relies on eyesight to catch prey. The visual part of the brain in the frog is larger than the part used for smell.

Human Brain

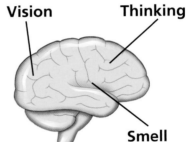

Vision   Thinking

Smell

In humans the region for vision is larger than that for smell. There is a large and developed region for thinking and memory.

Nervous System Facts

What: Nerve cells, spinal cord, brain

Where: Body network

Jobs: Control the senses; control muscles, breathing, heart rate, and many other body functions

Who has it: Vertebrates and almost all invertebrates

Special Sense Organs

Many animals have specialized sense organs that collect information about their surroundings. For example, a bat makes a series of clicking sounds, then listens for echo patterns when the clicks bounce off objects. Using echoes, it can find prey in the dark.

A snake's forked tongue collects tiny odor particles. These particles tell where prey or enemies are. The pictures show two more sense organs.

Lateral line

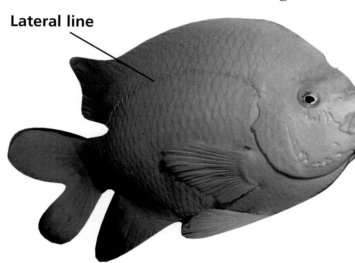

Cells along a fish's lateral line have tiny hairs. Waves in the water move the hairs. This helps the fish detect prey or enemies.

An insect eye has many lenses. Insects see light and movement in several directions, but not a clear image.

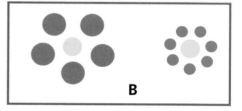

FOR SCHOOL OR HOME

Fool Your Senses

1. **Observe** Look at drawing A. What do you see?

2. **Observe** Study the center circles in drawing B. Which is larger?

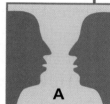

3. **Measure** Measure each center circle. Which is larger?

4. **Infer** Can your eyes fool you? Explain.

▷ **Why are sense organs important for an animal's survival?**

How Do Animals Move?

A vertebrate's bones form its **skeletal system** (SKEL·i·tuhl SIS·tuhm). Bones are living tissues. Minerals make bones hard. The skeletal system supports the body and protects body organs. It works with the **muscular system** (MUS·kyuh·luhr SIS·tum) to allow a vertebrate to move. The muscular system is made of the body's muscles. Muscles are tough tissues that can move.

How do invertebrates move? Almost all invertebrates that can move have some kind of muscle tissue. Muscles in an earthworm shorten and stretch to move the body.

In vertebrates muscles produce movement by shortening and

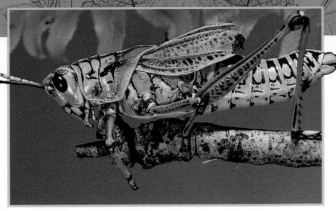

Muscles work in pairs to bend a joint, such as the joint in the middle of a grasshopper's leg. When one muscle shortens, it pulls on the joint. The other muscle in the pair relaxes and gets longer.

pulling on bones. Vertebrates use bones and muscles together to move in different ways. Powerful muscles allow a fish to wriggle back and forth as it swims. A snake uses its muscles to slither along. Its bones are designed to wriggle as its muscles shorten and relax.

Birds have powerful muscles in their chests. Some use them to fly at incredible speeds. A racing pigeon can fly at speeds of 177 kilometers (110 miles) per hour.

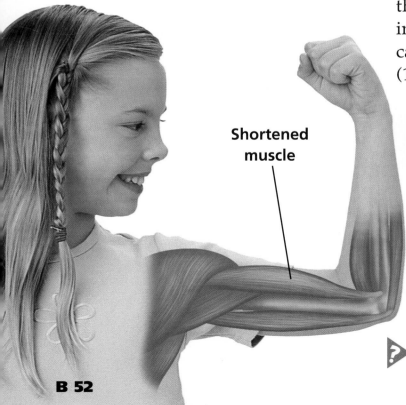

Shortened muscle

Muscular and Skeletal Systems Facts

What: Bones, muscles, cartilage
Where: Entire body
Jobs: Support, protect, move
Types: Exoskeleton and endoskeleton
Who has it: Vertebrates and some invertebrates
Works with: Nervous system

▷ **What do bones and muscles do?**

Why It Matters

Everything you do depends on organ systems. Think what happens when you kick a ball. Your nervous system sees the ball and sends a message to kick. Your circulatory system moves food and oxygen from your digestive and respiratory systems to your foot. Then your skeletal and muscular systems kick the ball! Stay healthy, and your body will keep working for you.

Think and Write

1. Name and describe the function of seven body systems. Which system controls all of the others?

2. Compare open and closed circulatory systems.

3. Describe three different ways that animals take in food.

4. Compare senses in three different animals.

5. **Critical Thinking** How are body systems different from one animal group to another? Which animals have simple body systems? More complex systems?

L·I·N·K·S

WRITING LINK

Write a paragraph. What if you could shrink to take a tour of one of your body systems? Describe which system you would choose and why.

ART LINK

Draw a picture. Describe what your tour of one of your body systems would be like. Draw pictures to add to your description.

MATH LINK

Measure your exercise. Work with a partner. Count how many times each of you breathes while you rest in a chair for a minute. Then take turns doing jumping jacks or running for one minute. Time your breathing again. Compare your results.

TECHNOLOGY LINK

 Science Newsroom CD-ROM Choose *At Arm's Length* to learn more about how your muscles work.

 At the Computer Visit **www.mhscience02.com** for more links.

Development and Reproduction

Process Skill

You **infer** when you form an idea from facts or observations.

Get Ready

What do you observe about these kittens? They have fur of different colors and patterns. However, they all have the same body size and shape. How do you think they will change as they grow?

Explore Activity

How Do Mealworms Change As They Grow?

Materials

jars containing food and mealworms in different stages of development

3 hand lenses

3 rulers

Procedure: Design Your Own

BE CAREFUL! Handle animals with care.

1. As a group, choose a Mealworm Observation Station that your teacher has set up. Each station has three jars labeled A, B, and C.

2. **Observe** Break into smaller groups. Each small group should observe the animals in one jar. Record your observations. Share your observations with the other members of your larger group.

3. Record any questions you have about mealworms and how they change and grow. How could you find the answers?

4. **Experiment** Design simple experiments to find out more about the mealworms. Do they prefer light or dark places? Damp or dry places?

5. **Observe** Make observations of the animals every few days. Record your observations.

Drawing Conclusions

1. **Communicate** Describe the stages of mealworm development.

2. Use your drawings to arrange the stages in the order in which you think mealworms develop.

3. **Going Further: Infer** How does the way a mealworm grows differ from how other animals like cats and dogs grow?

Main Idea Animals develop and reproduce in many different ways.

What Is Metamorphosis?

Most young animals look like smaller copies of their parents. Puppies look like small dogs. Chicks look like small birds. They grow larger as they grow older. However, other young animals don't look like their parents at all.

Certain animals, like mealworms, go through big changes during their development. This process is called **metamorphosis** (met·uh·MAWR·fuh·sis), meaning "a change in body form." There are two types of metamorphosis—complete and incomplete. Insects such as mealworms and butterflies go through complete metamorphosis.

Complete Metamorphosis

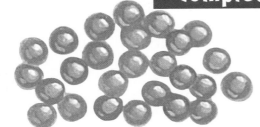

❶ Egg Stage
An adult mealworm is known as a grain beetle. After mating, a female grain beetle lays eggs.

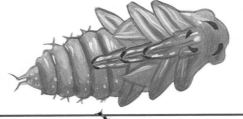

❷ Larva Stage
A wormlike *larva* (LAHR·vuh) hatches from each egg. A larva is a young organism with a form different from its parents. After hatching, a larva begins to eat.

❸ Pupa Stage
A larva becomes a *pupa* (PYEW·puh). Many changes take place in this stage. Adult tissues and organs form.

❹ Adult Stage
An adult grain beetle is completely unlike its larva. It has a smooth body, wings, and six legs.

Insects such as grasshoppers, termites, and damselflies go through incomplete metamorphosis. Metamorphosis allows animals to specialize. Larvae and nymphs specialize in eating and growing. Adult animals specialize in breeding. They come to a new environment where their eggs have a better chance of surviving.

▷ **How do nymphs differ from larvae?**

Metamorphosis

Complete stages	Incomplete stages
1. Egg 2. Larva 3. Pupa 4. Adult	1. Egg 2. Nymph 3. Adult
Time: several weeks	**Time** up to 2 years
Who does it: wasps, ants, bees, flies, beetles, fleas, butterflies, moths	**Who does it:** bugs, mayflies, dragonflies, grasshoppers, cockroaches, termites

Incomplete Metamorphosis

3 Adult Stage
The damselfly nymph molts several times until it becomes an adult.

2 Nymph Stage
The young damselfly, called a *nymph* (NIMF), hatches from an egg. A nymph is a young insect that looks like an adult. The damselfly *nymph* lives in water and has gills. After many weeks it comes out of the water. Soon it sheds its skin, or molts. Small wings appear.

1 Egg Stage
A female damselfly lays her eggs on a reed underwater.

READING

Diagrams

How do mealworms and damselflies change as they grow?

At what stage of life is each animal shown in these photographs?

What Are the Stages of an Animal's Life?

The mealworm goes through changes as it grows into an adult. These stages of growth and change make up an organism's **life cycle**.

Each different organism has its own particular life cycle. However, all organisms follow the same general pattern of birth, growth, reproduction, and death.

Humans have their own life cycle. Stages in the human life cycle are shown in the chart. Each person's life cycle is different. You may go through different stages at very different ages. Even so, all people have a life cycle that follows the same general pattern.

▷ **At what stage of the human life cycle are you?**

Human Life Cycle

Birth

Infancy
0–2 years

Childhood
3–12 years

Adolescence
13–18 years

Adulthood
19+ years

Death

How Long Do Animals Live?

The **life span** of an animal tells you how long it can be expected to live. The average life span of a human is about 75 to 80 years. Compare this with life spans of other organisms in the bar graph. Do you see any trends? Do certain animals live longer than others?

Scientists aren't sure what decides an animal's life span. They think cell division may control how long an animal lives.

Throughout an animal's life, its cells divide many times. Scientists think that after many divisions, cells get damaged. Older animals have more damaged cells than younger animals. Therefore, older animals are more likely to develop diseases that weaken them.

What might happen if scientists could slow down cell division? It is possible that animals—including people—could have longer life spans!

▷ **What is a life span?**

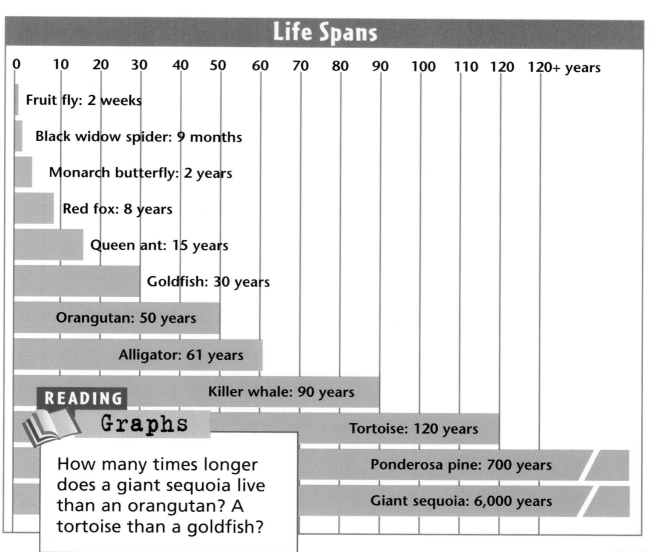

Life Spans

0 10 20 30 40 50 60 70 80 90 100 110 120 120+ years

Fruit fly: 2 weeks

Black widow spider: 9 months

Monarch butterfly: 2 years

Red fox: 8 years

Queen ant: 15 years

Goldfish: 30 years

Orangutan: 50 years

Alligator: 61 years

Killer whale: 90 years

Tortoise: 120 years

Ponderosa pine: 700 years

Giant sequoia: 6,000 years

READING Graphs

How many times longer does a giant sequoia live than an orangutan? A tortoise than a goldfish?

How Do Animals Reproduce?

The life cycle of every animal includes **reproduction** (ree·pruh·DUK·shuhn), the making of offspring. There are different ways animals can reproduce.

Budding and Regeneration

Simple invertebrates, like sponges and cnidarians, can reproduce by *budding*. A bud forms on the adult's body. It slowly develops into a new animal. After some time the bud breaks off. Each animal then continues its own life cycle.

In *regeneration* (ri·jen·uh·RAY·shuhn), a whole animal develops from just a part of the original animal. Sponges and planaria reproduce through regeneration.

Both budding and regeneration produce *clones*. A clone is an exact copy of its parent. Its traits, or characteristics, are identical to the traits of its parent.

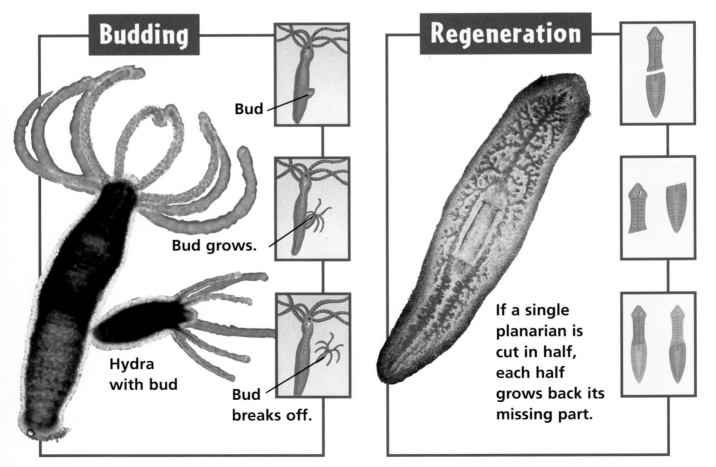

Budding

Bud

Bud grows.

Hydra with bud

Bud breaks off.

Regeneration

If a single planarian is cut in half, each half grows back its missing part.

Turtles are reptiles that lay eggs in protective shells. When an egg cell joins with a sperm cell, fertilization takes place. This produces a new organism.

Fertilization

Another type of reproduction requires cells from two parents. The female cell is called an *egg*. The male cell is called a *sperm*. Their offspring are not clones. They are similar to their parents but not identical. These offspring are new individuals. They have traits from both parents.

Do you think an egg can become a new organism by itself? In most cases it cannot. Neither can a sperm. To reproduce, an egg and a sperm join. This joining is called *fertilization* (fur·tuh·luh·ZAY·shuhn). This produces a developing animal called an *embryo* (EM·bree·oh). An embryo can grow to become a new organism, with traits from both parents.

Some animals lay eggs. Egg-laying animals include most invertebrates, reptiles, amphibians, birds, fish, and a very few mammals. In most cases the embryo grows inside a protective shell. The embryo uses stored food in the egg to develop. After maturing, the offspring hatches into a newborn animal.

All but a few mammals give birth to live young. One mammal that lays eggs is the platypus.

READING **Main Idea**

What are three ways that animals reproduce?

Comparing Reproduction

	Budding and Regeneration	Fertilization
Parents	1	2
Male and female	no	yes
Clones	yes	no
Offspring traits	same as parent	mixed
Egg and sperm	no	yes

QUICK LAB

FOR SCHOOL OR HOME

Heredity Cards

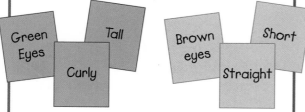

Green Eyes

Tall

Curly

Brown eyes

Short

Straight

1. Cut three cards from each paper. Pink cards represent the female, blue cards the male.

2. Write a trait for "Hair," "Eye color," and "Height" on one set of cards. Make sure the traits on the other set are different.

3. Match cards to make "offspring." Each offspring needs one card for each trait.

4. Continue matching cards to create offspring. Give each a number. Record the traits in a table.

5. **Observe** How many different offspring did you get?

6. **Predict** How many offspring would you get with eight cards?

How Are Traits Passed to Offspring?

The passing of traits from parent to offspring is called **heredity** (huh·RED·i·tee). Offspring inherit traits from both parents.

When an egg and a sperm join, the traits they carry are mixed like a deck of cards. The offspring ends up with a mixture of traits. Some traits come from the father. Other traits come from the mother.

Farmers learned long ago that they could choose and mate, or breed, animals with desirable traits. They bred sheep with longer hair or corn with many juicy ears on one stalk.

▶ **How do farmers use heredity?**

A cow raised for its milk

A sheep bred for longer, thicker hair

L·I·N·K·S

Why It Matters

Where are you in your life cycle right now? You are probably in the childhood stage. In a few years, you'll reach adolescence, then adulthood. What challenges lie ahead for you? What dangers and opportunities? Knowing about life cycles can help you identify some of the problems that lie ahead and plan for a better future. What plans do you have for your adolescent years? What can you do now to help you achieve your goals?

Think and Write

1. What is the difference between a life cycle and a life span?

2. Compare complete and incomplete metamorphosis.

3. What is heredity?

4. How is budding different from fertilization?

5. **Critical Thinking** Do you think that animals should be bred to develop specific traits? Why or why not?

WRITING LINK

Write a plan. What would you like to accomplish in your adult years? Why? Write a plan for how you would like to achieve your goals.

ART LINK

Make a collage. Find pictures of animals and their young. Clip them from magazines, or copy them from books or the Internet. Arrange the pictures into a collage. Add words to explain how young compare with their parents.

HEALTH LINK

Write a paragraph. The average human life span has increased a lot since the 1800s. Back then, it was only 35 or 40 years. Why do you think people now live twice as long? List some reasons.

TECHNOLOGY LINK

Science Newsroom CD-ROM Choose *Don't Bug Me* to learn how to tell butterflies and moths apart.

At the Computer Visit **www.mhscience02.com** for more links.

Animal Survival

Vocabulary

camouflage, B66

adaptation, B66

mimicry, B68

inherited behavior, B70

instinct, B70

learned behavior, B71

Get Ready

Have you ever played hide-and-seek? Where did you hide? How did you cover yourself up? The insect in this picture is also hiding. Why might larger animals have trouble seeing it?

Process Skill

You predict when you state possible results from an event or experiment.

Explore Activity

How Can Body Color Help an Animal Survive?

Materials

colored toothpicks

plastic bag or shoe box

label or piece of masking tape

marking pen

Procedure

1. Label your bag or box with your name. This is your "nest." Use it to hold all the toothpick "worms" that you collect.

2. **Observe** Follow the rules given by your teacher to capture the worms. Record the rules. Also record any observations that you make while collecting the worms.

3. **Communicate** When you are done, record your results in a bar graph like the one shown.

Drawing Conclusions

1. Which color worms were easiest to see? Why?

2. Which color worms were hardest to see? Why?

3. If you were to become a toothpick worm, what color would you want to be? Why?

4. **Going further: Predict** Colors help certain animals blend in with their surroundings. Why do you think some animals have bright colors? How could you find out?

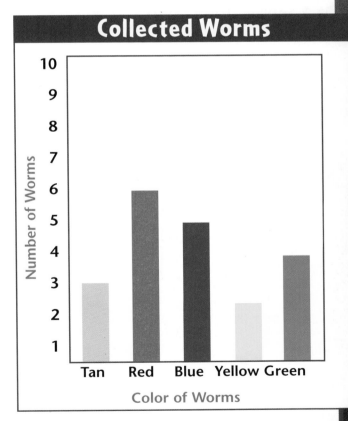

Collected Worms

Number of Worms

Tan Red Blue Yellow Green

Color of Worms

Main Idea Body parts help an animal survive.

What Are Adaptations?

An animal's color can help it blend into its surroundings. Blending due to color is called **camouflage** (KAM·uh·flahzh).

In the early 1800s, dark peppered moths were rare in England. Light moths were common. Then factories polluted England's air in the late 1800s. Suddenly dark moths outnumbered light moths.

Why do you think that happened? Dark moths stood out on light-colored trees. Birds could spot them

You can see the leaf mimic among dark-colored leaves, but in nature the insect is the same color as the leaves.

easily and ate them. Then pollution slowly darkened the trees. The light moths stood out and were eaten.

Look at the picture above. That isn't a leaf—it's an insect! Its body resembles its environment very closely. This is *protective resemblance* (pruh·TEK·tiv ri·ZEM·bluhns). The fact that an animal resembles something else protects it.

Camouflage and protective resemblance are examples of **adaptations** (ad·uhp·TAY·shuhnz). Adaptations are traits that help organisms survive.

Light and dark peppered moths.

Body adaptations are called physical adaptations. Physical adaptations help animals survive in their environments. Here are just a few physical adaptations.

- **Gills and Fins** They allow fish to breathe and swim underwater.

- **Fur** Thick white fur helps a polar bear blend in with its snowy home. It also keeps the bear warm.

- **Legs** The long legs of the horse help it run fast.

- **Neck** A giraffe's long legs and neck allow it to reach leaves high up in trees, where other animals can't reach.

- **Shell** A hard outer shell protects a turtle's soft body parts.

- **Trunk** A trunk helps an elephant grasp things, and feed itself.

- **Bright Color** The bright red body of a male cardinal helps it attract a mate. In other animals bright colors tell predators to stay away. They have learned the animal is poisonous!

Animal adaptations happen naturally. The peppered moths didn't choose to be dark or light. The birds simply ate the light-colored moths because they were easier to see on the dark trees. Only an adaptation that helps an animal survive is likely to become common.

This giraffe can reach leaves high up in trees.

READING Main Idea

What are three animal adaptations?

What Is Mimicry?

Monarch butterflies have an important adaptation that helps them survive—they don't taste good. Predators spit out monarch butterflies if they eat them. Monarch butterfly bodies contain a poison that they get from feeding on the milkweed plant.

Most predators stay away from monarch butterflies. They recognize the bold, bright coloring. Predators also stay away from the viceroy butterfly. The viceroy is not poisonous, nor does it taste bad. However, it looks very similar to the monarch. Most predators won't take a chance eating it.

The viceroy butterfly is protected by **mimicry** (MIM·i·kree). Mimicry occurs when one organism imitates another. What advantage does mimicry give animals?

How did the viceroy come to resemble the bad-tasting monarch? At one time there probably was a variety of viceroy butterflies. The ones that looked like monarchs survived. The ones that looked less like monarchs got eaten. As time passed, the viceroys that looked more and more like monarchs survived.

▷ **How does mimicry help the viceroy butterfly survive?**

Monarch butterfly

Viceroy butterfly

Process Skill
BUILDER

 **SKILL** Form a Hypothesis

How Do Adaptations Help an Animal Survive?

Every science experiment begins with a hypothesis. A hypothesis is a statement you can test. "Dogs like big bones best" is a hypothesis. You could test this hypothesis by giving dogs different-sized bones.

In this activity you will design two different kinds of animals— a super predator and an animal that is skilled at avoiding predators. Then form a hypothesis about how their adaptations would help each animal in different situations.

Materials

modeling clay

construction paper

drawing materials

Procedure

1 What traits should your predator have? Record them. Describe how these traits would help the animal.

2 Do the same for your avoider animal.

3 **Communicate** Make a table like the one shown for each animal. Fill in each category that applies. Add any extra categories that you need.

4 **Make a Model** Make models or colored drawings of your animals. Label all the features of your animals. Tell how they function.

5 **Form a Hypothesis** How would these features help the animal survive?

Drawing Conclusions

1 **Communicate** What are the animals' most important features? How would they use these features?

2 Review your hypothesis. How could you test it?

3 **Predict** Predict what would happen if you could test your hypothesis.

Animal Name _____	
Predator ☐　　　　 Avoider ☐	
Food _____	
Enemies _____	
Environment _____	
Trait	**How It Helps**
Length	
Weight	
Shape	
Coloring	
Pattern	
Skin	
Arms	
Legs	
Tails	
Fins	
Eyesight	
Hearing	
Smell	
Strength	
Quickness	
Intelligence	

How Do Animals Behave?

Physical adaptations help animals survive. Other kinds of adaptations involve behaviors, or actions.

One type of behavior is not learned. It is an **inherited behavior** (in·HER·it·uhd bi·HAYV·yuhr). The simplest inherited behavior is a *reflex* (REE·fleks). A reflex is automatic, like scratching an itch.

Complicated inherited behavior is called **instinct** (IN·stingkt). Instincts are patterns of behavior, like spinning a web and building a nest. The behavior is complicated, but automatic. The spider and bird do not think about what to do, they just know.

When salmon swim thousands of miles to mate and lay eggs, they are *migrating* (MIGH·grayt·ing). Migration is an instinct. Animals migrate for three main reasons. First, they avoid cold weather. Second, they find new food supplies. Third, they find a safe place to breed and raise their young.

How do migrating animals find their way? Many birds navigate by the Sun and the stars. Other migrators may use magnetic "compasses" inside their bodies.

A spider knows how to spin a web because of instinct.

Surviving a cold winter is hard. Some animals struggle to find food. Others *hibernate* (HIGH·buhr·nayt), or sleep through the winter. True hibernation is a deep sleep. All body processes slow down. Body temperature can drop to just above freezing. Mice and bats are true hibernators.

Bears and chipmunks do not sleep as deeply. Their body temperatures drop, but their heartbeats remain high. They can wake up in an emergency.

The dormouse is a true hibernator. It loses up to half its body weight while hibernating.

Some animal behaviors are inherited. Others aren't. Behavior that is not inborn is called **learned behavior**. Animals learn through experience and change their behavior. Learning starts with a need, such as food, protection, and escaping predators. All animals do not learn in the same way.

- **Learning to Ignore** At first a frog jumps at moving shadows. Later it doesn't. It has learned that the shadow is not a threat.
- **Copying** Newborn ducks follow their female parent wherever she goes. They copy her to learn to find food.
- **Learning from Experience** At first a rat is unsure of where to go in a maze. After many trips the rat learns to find its way from experience.
- **Using Two Unrelated Things** A trainer shouts, "Up!" If the dolphin jumps, the trainer gives it a fish. At first the dolphin gets a fish every time it jumps. After a while it jumps simply because the trainer shouts, "Up!"

Almost all learning involves some form of trial and error. For example, the rat in the maze makes mistakes but learns from them. After a while it can find its way through the maze.

A program called Helping Hands trains monkeys, then places them

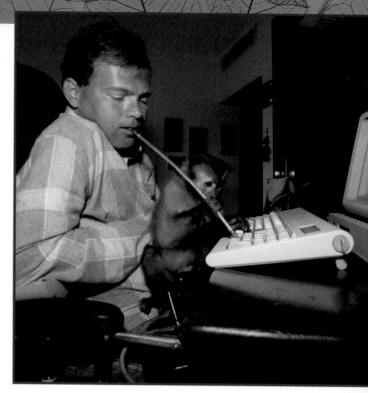

This monkey helps its owner live a better life. It is a companion and a helper.

with people who have trouble moving their bodies. What do Helping Hands monkeys do? They open books and fetch snacks. They change radio and TV stations. They perform dozens of tasks quickly and easily.

Many animals are trained to help people. Dogs can be trained to help the blind. Horses are trained to carry people on their backs.

▷ **What are some of your inherited behaviors and learned behaviors?**

How Can Quick Responses Help Animals Survive?

Many types of animals have special behaviors that help them survive. For example, when a squid senses danger, it squirts a dark, inky liquid at an attacker. The liquid blinds the attacker for a short time and lessens its sense of smell. This allows the squid to make a quick getaway.

A puffer fish has a body covered with sharp, hard spines. When attacked or scared, the puffer fish inflates its body to look like a ball. This pushes the sharp, hard spines outward.

Another prickly animal is the porcupine. It has specialized hairs called *quills*. About 30,000 hard, sharp quills with barbed ends cover a porcupine's body and tail. When the porcupine is attacked, the hairs stand up to protect the animal's body. Also, a porcupine can slap an attacker with its tail, sending painfully sharp quills into the attacker's body.

Puffer fish

Have you ever smelled a skunk? A skunk protects itself by spraying a terrible-smelling liquid at attackers. This liquid is also very painful when it gets into the eyes.

Some animals use their outer body coverings as a shield. An insect called a sow bug can roll itself into a ball. Its hard outer covering protects it from enemies. Two types of mammals, armadillos and pangolins, have hard protective plates. Like sow bugs, they roll into a ball to protect themselves.

Armadillo

Porcupine

▶ **What quick responses do these animals use to survive?**

L·I·N·K·S

Why It Matters

Understanding adaptations helps us learn how animals survive. It also makes us more aware of our own adaptations—our hands, feet, eyes, nose, ears, and tongue to name a few. Your greatest adaptation of all is your brain. It can produce more learned behavior than any other organism. In fact, you are using it right now—to learn! Visit **www.mhscience02.com** to do a research project on animal adaptations.

Think and Write

1. How is camouflage different from mimicry? How do both help animals survive?

2. What is an instinct?

3. Describe how a dog might learn to open the cabinet where its food is kept.

4. Form a Hypothesis How might having a bright color help a bird survive?

5. Critical Thinking A sheepdog is an expert at herding sheep. Do you think this is learned or inherited behavior? Why?

LITERATURE LINK

Read *Why Tortoise Has a Shell* to learn how Tortoise found a way to protect and shelter herself. Try the activities at the end of the book.

WRITING LINK

Write a paragraph. Choose an adaptation you would like to have. Why would you choose that adaptation? How would it help you in your life?

SOCIAL STUDIES LINK

Research bears. Research where brown bears and polar bears live. Explain how their appearance is related to their environment.

TECHNOLOGY LINK

Science Newsroom CD-ROM Choose *A Change for the Better* to learn how beaks help birds obtain food.

At the Computer Visit **www.mhscience02.com** for more links.

Dancing Bees

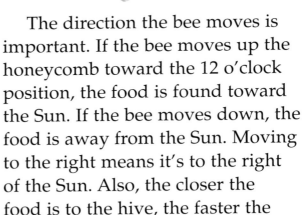

Most types of honeybees collect nectar, the sweet juice of a flower, and pollen. When one bee finds a good source of pollen and nectar, it flies back to its hive to tell all the others.

How do you think some types of honeybees communicate this information? Scientists have been studying honeybee communication for a long time. They observed that bees perform a special type of "waggle" dance. Even the Greek philosopher Aristotle, who lived from 384 to 322 B.C., observed honeybee dances!

Scientists have used a variety of experiments to learn how bees communicate with each other. After a bee finds a flower, it first fills its honey sac with nectar and returns to the hive. There it performs a special dance. As the bee walks in a figure eight, it stops from time to time to shake, or waggle, its body.

The direction the bee moves is important. If the bee moves up the honeycomb toward the 12 o'clock position, the food is found toward the Sun. If the bee moves down, the food is away from the Sun. Moving to the right means it's to the right of the Sun. Also, the closer the food is to the hive, the faster the bee moves.

For a long time, scientists thought that bees communicated only by dancing. They now know that some bees also use sounds created by beating their wings. Through experiments, they found that dancing alone doesn't communicate the food's location. The other bees didn't look for the food. However, when the bees were allowed to hear the correct sounds from the dancer's beating wings, they flew straight to the food. Who would have thought that bees can hear!

Write ABOUT IT

1. How do bees communicate with each other?

2. How does a bee tell other bees in the hive that food is found toward the Sun?

AT THE COMPUTER

Visit www.mhscience02.com to learn more about bees.

Chapter 4 Review

Vocabulary

Fill each blank with the best word or words from the list.

adaptation, B66
camouflage, B66
circulatory system, B46
excretory system, B47
heredity, B62
instinct, B70

learned behavior, B71
life cycle, B58
nervous system, B50
respiratory system, B47

1. The organ system that removes liquid wastes is called the _____.

2. The stages of an animal's growth and change are part of its _____.

3. Organisms use _____ to blend with their surroundings.

4. The system that moves blood through the body is the _____.

5. All body systems are controlled by the _____.

6. The passing of a trait from parents to offspring is _____.

7. A pattern of behavior that an animal is born with is called a(n) _____.

8. Species have often survived changing environments through _____.

9. Some animals take in gases through their skin, and lack a(n) _____.

10. When a dog plays dead, it is showing a(n) _____.

Test Prep

11. The system that carries oxygen to body cells is the _____.

    A circulatory system
    B respiratory system
    C excretory system
    D digestive system

12. Which animal goes through metamorphosis?

    F mealworm
    G chicken
    H snake
    J fish

13. A robin's beak helps it to catch worms. Its beak shape is a(n) _____.

    A adaptation

    B instinct

    C learned behavior

    D mimicry

14. When a bear hibernates, it _____.

    F eats food

    G catches fish

    H climbs trees

    J does none of these things

15. Which of these processes helps species become more diverse?

    A regeneration

    B respiration

    C fertilization

    D budding

Concepts and Skills

16. **Reading in Science** Name three adaptations that help animals survive. Describe how these adaptations help the animals.

17. **Decision Making** Humans can decide what to learn and how to learn it. What would you like to learn, and why? Discuss the ways you learn something new.

18. **Process Skills:** Form a Hypothesis Most birds build nests, where they live and raise their young. Does a bird learn how to build nests, or is it an instinct? Form a hypothesis. Then design an experiment to answer this question.

19. **Safety** Why is it important to handle living animals carefully?

20. **Critical Thinking** Compare how camouflage and mimicry protect an animal. Use examples in your answer.

Boost your test scores!

Be Smart! Visit www.mhscience02.com to learn more.

People in Science

Dr. Coretta Patterson
Veterinarian

Do you have a pet? What do you do when it gets sick? Sometimes it's hard to tell when animals are sick. They can't tell you exactly what's wrong. Sometimes you know they're sick, but you don't know what to do. That's when you need to take your pet to the veterinarian. A veterinarian, or vet, is a special doctor just for animals.

There are different kinds of vets. Some treat small animals like dogs and cats. Some treat large animals like the horses and cows on a farm. Some do not treat animals at all but do veterinary research in a laboratory.

Dr. Coretta Patterson is a veterinarian at Michigan State University College of Veterinary Medicine. She had wanted to become a vet since she was a child and spent summers on a family farm in Alabama. Veterinarians must attend veterinary school for about four years after completing college. Dr. Patterson received her doctorate of veterinary medicine from the University of Illinois.

Dr. Patterson treats animals at the university's animal clinic.

Animal Pages

Your goal is to make a page for a book about animals.

What to Do

1. Choose an animal to research. Find answers to the following questions:

- How is the animal classified?
- What is the animal's body like?
- Where does the animal live?
- Where does it fit in a food chain or food web?
- Is the animal endangered?

2. Write the animal's name and your name at the top of a sheet of paper. Use the rest of the sheet to present the information you learned about the animal. Include words and pictures.

3. With your classmates, staple or tape the pages together to make a book. Include a cover and a table of contents.

Animal Tale

What to Do

Write a story or play about an animal or group of animals. The point of view could be that of someone studying animals or that of the animals themselves.

Your story or play should answer at least one of these questions:

- How does an animal change as it grows?
- How does it use adaptations to stay alive?
- What happens when its habitat changes or is destroyed?

The Claw of the Tiger by Mary B.

Her usual duties include checkups, blood tests, dental work, and shots—ouch! She gets help from her nurse and technician. A veterinary technician is an assistant. Technicians go to school for about two years to get their degree. They assist vets in many ways, but they are not doctors.

Dr. Patterson also teaches classes for future vets. She enjoys teaching because it allows her to encourage students to pursue a meaningful profession. She loves her job because she feels she's making a real difference!

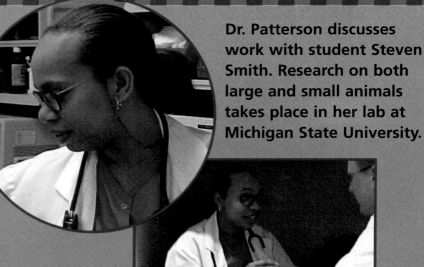

Dr. Patterson discusses work with student Steven Smith. Research on both large and small animals takes place in her lab at Michigan State University.

AT THE COMPUTER

Visit www.mhscience02.com to learn more about careers.

Write ABOUT IT

1. Describe two different kinds of work veterinarians do.
2. How do you think being a veterinarian is different from being a physician?

Careers IN SCIENCE

Here are some different types of careers related to the study of veterinary medicine. You can use the Internet or library resources to find out more about these careers.

- veterinary technician
- naturalist
- zoologist
- biologist
- physician

As you study science, you will learn many new words. You will read about many new ideas. Read these pages. They will help you understand this book.

1. The **Vocabulary** list has all the new words you will learn in the lesson. The page numbers tell you where the words are taught.

2. The name tells you what the lesson is about.

3. **Get Ready** uses the picture on the page to help you start thinking about the lesson.

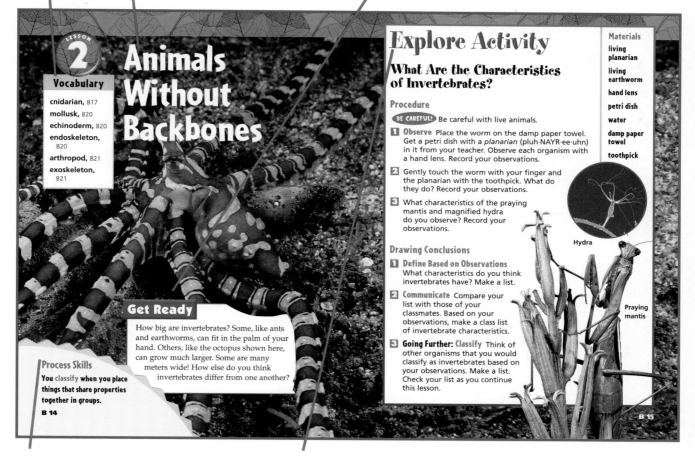

LESSON 2

Animals Without Backbones

Vocabulary

cnidarian, B17
mollusk, B20
echinoderm, B20
endoskeleton, B20
arthropod, B21
exoskeleton, B21

Get Ready

How big are invertebrates? Some, like ants and earthworms, can fit in the palm of your hand. Others, like the octopus shown here, can grow much larger. Some are many meters wide! How else do you think invertebrates differ from one another?

Process Skills

You classify when you place things that share properties together in groups.

B 14

Explore Activity

What Are the Characteristics of Invertebrates?

Materials

living planarian
living earthworm
hand lens
petri dish
water
damp paper towel
toothpick

Procedure

BE CAREFUL! Be careful with live animals.

1 Observe Place the worm on the damp paper towel. Get a petri dish with a *planarian* (pluh-NAYR-ee-uhn) in it from your teacher. Observe each organism with a hand lens. Record your observations.

2 Gently touch the worm with your finger and the planarian with the toothpick. What do they do? Record your observations.

3 What characteristics of the praying mantis and magnified hydra do you observe? Record your observations.

Hydra

Drawing Conclusions

1 Define Based on Observations What characteristics do you think invertebrates have? Make a list.

2 Communicate Compare your list with those of your classmates. Based on your observations, make a class list of invertebrate characteristics.

Praying mantis

3 Going Further: Classify Think of other organisms that you would classify as invertebrates based on your observations. Make a list. Check your list as you continue this lesson.

B 15

4. This **Process Skill** is used in the Explore Activity.

5. The **Explore Activity** is a hands-on way to learn about the lesson .

As you read a lesson, follow these three steps. They will help you to understand what you are reading.

1. This box contains the Main Idea of the lesson. Keep the main idea of the lesson in mind as you read.

2. Before Reading Read the large red question before you read the page. Try to answer this question from what you already know.

3. During Reading Look for new Vocabulary words in yellow. Look at the pictures. They will help you understand what you are reading.

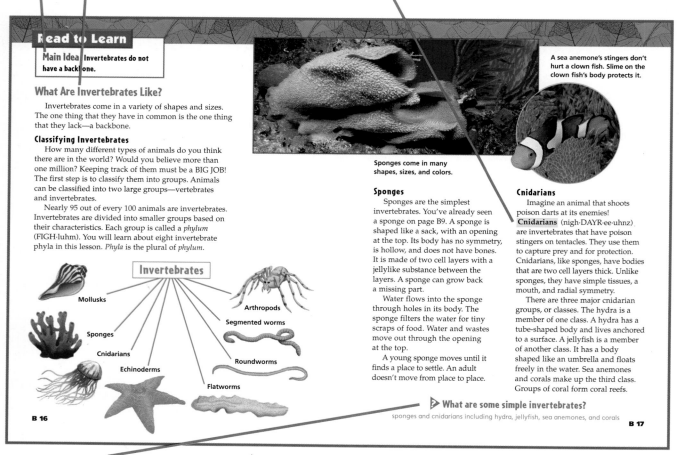

Read to Learn

Main Idea Invertebrates do not have a backbone.

What Are Invertebrates Like?

Invertebrates come in a variety of shapes and sizes. The one thing that they have in common is the one thing that they lack—a backbone.

Classifying Invertebrates

How many different types of animals do you think there are in the world? Would you believe more than one million? Keeping track of them must be a BIG JOB! The first step is to classify them into groups. Animals can be classified into two large groups—vertebrates and invertebrates.

Nearly 95 out of every 100 animals are invertebrates. Invertebrates are divided into smaller groups based on their characteristics. Each group is called a *phylum* (FIGH·luhm). You will learn about eight invertebrate phyla in this lesson. *Phyla* is the plural of *phylum*.

Invertebrates

Mollusks
Sponges
Cnidarians
Echinoderms
Arthropods
Segmented worms
Roundworms
Flatworms

B 16

A sea anemone's stingers don't hurt a clown fish. Slime on the clown fish's body protects it.

Sponges come in many shapes, sizes, and colors.

Sponges

Sponges are the simplest invertebrates. You've already seen a sponge on page B9. A sponge is shaped like a sack, with an opening at the top. Its body has no symmetry, is hollow, and does not have bones. It is made of two cell layers with a jellylike substance between the layers. A sponge can grow back a missing part.

Water flows into the sponge through holes in its body. The sponge filters the water for tiny scraps of food. Water and wastes move out through the opening at the top.

A young sponge moves until it finds a place to settle. An adult doesn't move from place to place.

Cnidarians

Imagine an animal that shoots poison darts at its enemies! **Cnidarians** (nigh·DAYR·ee·uhnz) are invertebrates that have poison stingers on tentacles. They use them to capture prey and for protection. Cnidarians, like sponges, have bodies that are two cell layers thick. Unlike sponges, they have simple tissues, a mouth, and radial symmetry.

There are three major cnidarian groups, or classes. The hydra is a member of one class. A hydra has a tube-shaped body and lives anchored to a surface. A jellyfish is a member of another class. It has a body shaped like an umbrella and floats freely in the water. Sea anemones and corals make up the third class. Groups of coral form coral reefs.

▷ What are some simple invertebrates?
sponges and cnidarians including hydra, jellyfish, sea anemones, and corals

B 17

4. After Reading ▷ This arrow points to a question. It will help you check that you understand what you have read. Try to answer the question before you go to the next large red question.

Sumerians, F20
Sun, C80–81, F15
    as heat source, F38
    as star, C80–81
    movement of, C65*–66
    satellites of, C81
    tides and, D30
Sunlight, A41*, A42
Supernova, E21
Surface area and evaporation,
    D44*
Surface currents, D29
Surface waves, C57
Survival, animal, B64–75
    adaptations for, B66–67, B69*
    behaviors for, B70–72
    body color and, B65*–66, B67
    mimicry, B68
Swamps, D8
Swift, B33
Switch, F78–79
Symmetry, animal, B8–10

Tadpole, B31
Taiga, A44
Talc, C7, C8
Tapeworm, B18
Taproot, A71
Tarantulas, B38–39
Tarnish, E53
Tar pits, fossils in, C20
Telescopes, C76–77
Temperature
    heat vs., F35
    of air, D66, D72
    precipitation and, D19
Terminals, electric, F81
Terminus, C34, C35
Texture, C46, E45
Thermal energy, F15
Thermometer, D72, F35
Thermosphere, D65
Third–class lever, F23
Thunderstorms, D90
Tides, D30–31
Tilt meter, C59

Tissues, A14, A15
Titan arum flower of Sumatra,
    A78–79
Titanic, C32
Toad, B31
Tools for hearing, F60. *See also*
    Machines.
Topsoil, C45
Tornadoes, D90–91
Tortoises, B32
Traits, A21, B62
Transformers, F96
Translucency, F49
Transparency, F49
Transpiration, A73, D41
Trenches, D7
Tropical rain forest. *See* Rain
    forests.
Troposphere, D65
Trough of wave, D32, D33
Trunk, B67
Tuataras, B32
Tube feet, B20, B48
Tundra, A44
Turbine, F95
Turtles, B32, B61
Twisters, D90–91
Tyrannosaurus rex, A28

Ultraviolet light, D74–75, F42–43
Underground water sources, D10,
    D11
Universe, views of, C90–91
Uranus, C84, C85

Vacuole, A9
Valleys under water, D7
Van de Graaf generator, F68
Variables, using, A80, D44*, D62, F4
Vegetation, D39
Veins, A73, A74
Venus, C82, C83

Venus flytrap, A78–79
Vertebrates, A33, B8, B16, B26–35
    amphibians, B28, B31, B45*,
        B47
    birds, B28, B33, B48, B49
    bony fish, B28, B29, B30
    cartilaginous fish, B28, B29, B30
    characteristics of, B27*–28
    classifying, B26, B28–35*
    jawless fish, B28, B29
    mammals, B28, B34–35
    muscular system of, B52
    reptiles, B28, B32
Veterinarians, B78–79
Vibrations, sound and, F53*–55
Viceroy butterfly, B68
Vinegar eel, B18
Viruses, A16
Visible spectrum, F42–43
Volcanic glass, C9
Volt, F96
Voltage, F96
Volume, E17–18*
Vonnegut, Bernard, D25

Walruses, F32
Warm–blooded animals, B28
Warm fronts, D80, D81, D83
Wastes, B49, D51
Water, D4–26, D36–61, E37
    cleaning up, D52
    climate and bodies of, D86
    condensation of, D17, D19,
        D20, D21
    conservation of, D54
    desalination of, D56–57
    effect on ecosystems, A42
    erosion by, C38, C40–41
    evaporation of, D15*–17,
        D18*, D19, D20, D21, D44*
    flow through rocks, D37*–38
    flow through soil, C48*–49,
        D37*–38
    freezing of, D19, D20
    fresh, D47*, D48–50, D55
    in an apple, D12*

in living things, D12
plants' role in moving, D12, D41
pollution of, A58, A60, D51
precipitation, D18–19, D21,
    D22, D24, D39*, D43
sources of, D5*–11, D16–17
states of, E46–47
turbines powered by, F95
volume of solid measured
    using, E17
wasted, D54*
wells, D40
Water cycle, D20–21, D41
Water pressure, D67
Water table, D38, D39
Water treatment plants, D52
Water vapor, D6, D17, D19, D64,
    D78
clouds and, D71
Wavelength, D32, F42–43
Waves

ocean, C38, D32*–34
sound, F55, F58–59
Weather, D66–69
air masses and, D79–81
describing, D72
predicting, D82–83
storms, D90–91
Weather maps, D82–83
Weather vane, D72
Weathering, C13
Wedges, F20, F27
Weight, E19, F12
Wells, D40
Westerlies, D87
Wet cells, F81
Wheels and axles, F20, F25
Wind, D67–69
cause of, D68–69
climate and, D87
erosion by, C38, C40–41
global, D87

measuring, D72
waves and, D33
Wind turbines, F95
Wood, as insulator, F34
Woodland forest, A42–43
Woody stems, A72
Woolly mammoths, A34, A62–63
Work, F13
Worms, B16, B18, B19, B49

X rays, F42–43
Xylem cells, A72

Yeast, A13

*Indicates an activity rela‿

Measurement

Volume of Fluids

1. This bottle of juice has a volume of 1 liter.

2. That is a little more than 1 quart.

3. I weigh 85 pounds. That is a force of 380.8 newtons.

Weight/ Force

Rate

1. She can walk 20 meters in 5 seconds.

2. That means her speed is 4 meters per second.

Table of Measurements

SI (International System) of Units	English System of Units
Temperature Water freezes at 0 degrees Celsius (°C) and boils at 100°C.	**Temperature** Water freezes at 32 degrees Fahrenheit (°F) and boils at 212°F.
Length and Distance 10 millimeters (mm) = 1 centimeter (cm) 100 centimeters = 1 meter (m) 1,000 meters = 1 kilometer (km)	**Length and Distance** 12 inches (in.) = 1 foot (ft) 3 feet = 1 yard (yd) 5,280 feet = 1 mile (mi)
Volume 1 cubic centimeter (cm^3) = 1 milliliter (mL) 1,000 milliliters = 1 liter (L)	**Volume of Fluids** 8 fluid ounces (fl oz) = 1 cup (c) 2 cups = 1 pint (pt) 2 pints = 1 quart (qt) 4 quarts = 1 gallon (gal)
Mass 1,000 milligrams (mg) = 1 gram (g) 1,000 grams = 1 kilogram (kg)	**Weight** 16 ounces (oz) = 1 pound (lb) 2,000 pounds = 1 ton (T)
Area 1 square kilometer (km^2) = 1 km x 1 km 1 hectare = 10,000 square meters (m^2)	**Rate** mph = miles per hour
Rate m/s = meters per second km/h = kilometers per hour	
Force 1 newton (N) = 1 kg x 1m/s^2	

Use a Hand Lens

You use a hand lens to magnify an object, or make the object look larger. With a hand lens, you can see details that would be hard to see without the hand lens.

Magnify a Piece of Cereal

1. Place a piece of your favorite cereal on a flat surface. Look at the cereal carefully. Draw a picture of it.

2. Hold the hand lens so that it is just above the cereal. Look through the lens, and slowly move it away from the cereal. The cereal will look larger.

3. Keep moving the hand lens until the cereal begins to look blurry. Then move the lens a little closer to the cereal until you can see it clearly.

4. Draw a picture of the cereal as you see it through the hand lens. Fill in details that you did not see before.

5. Repeat this activity using objects you are studying in science. It might be a rock, some soil, a seed, or something else.

Collect Data

Use a Microscope

Hand lenses make objects look several times larger. A microscope, however, can magnify an object to look hundreds of times larger.

Examine Salt Grains

1. Place the microscope on a flat surface. Always carry a microscope with both hands. Hold the arm with one hand, and put your other hand beneath the base.
2. Look at the drawing to learn the different parts of the microscope.
3. Move the mirror so that it reflects light up toward the stage. Never point the mirror directly at the Sun or a bright light. Bright light can cause permanent eye damage.
4. Place a few grains of salt on the slide. Put the slide under the stage clips on the stage. Be sure that the salt grains are over the hole in the stage.
5. Look through the eyepiece. Turn the focusing knob slowly until the salt grains come into focus.
6. Draw what the grains look like through the microscope.
7. Look at other objects through the microscope. Try a piece of leaf, a strand of human hair, or a pencil mark.
8. Draw what each object looks like through the microscope. Do any of the objects look alike? If so, how? Are any of the objects alive? How do you know?

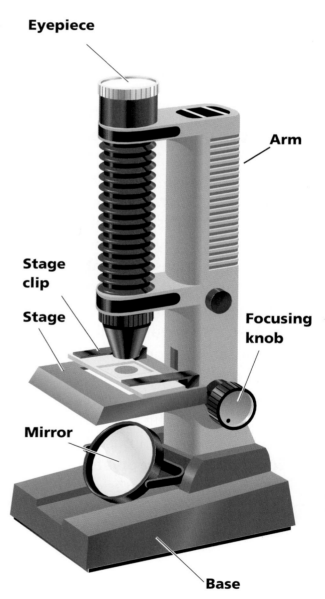

Eyepiece

Arm

Stage clip

Stage

Focusing knob

Mirror

Base

Measure Time

You use timing devices to measure how long something takes to happen. Some timing devices you use in science are a clock with a second hand and a stopwatch. Which one is more accurate?

Comparing a Clock and a Stopwatch

1. Look at a clock with a second hand. The second hand is the hand that you can see moving. It measures seconds.
2. Get an egg timer with falling sand. When the second hand of the clock points to 12, tell your partner to start the egg timer. Watch the clock while the sand in the egg timer is falling.
3. When the sand stops falling, count how many seconds it took. Record this measurement. Repeat the activity, and compare the two measurements.
4. Look at a stopwatch. Click the button on the top right. This starts the time. Click the button again. This stops the time. Click the button on the top left. This sets the stopwatch back to zero. Notice that the stopwatch tells time in hours, minutes, seconds, and hundredths of a second.
5. Repeat the activity in steps 1–3, but use the stopwatch instead of a clock. Make sure the stopwatch is set to zero. Click the top right button to start timing. Click the

button again when the sand stops falling. Make sure you and your partner time the sand twice.

0 minutes   **25 seconds 72 hundredths of a second**

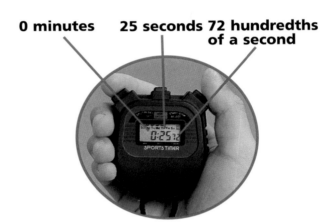

More About Time

1. Use the stopwatch to time how long it takes an ice cube to melt under cold running water. How long does an ice cube take to melt under warm running water?
2. Match each of these times with the action you think took that amount of time.

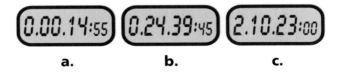

a.   b.   c.

1. A Little League baseball game
2. Saying the Pledge of Allegiance
3. Recess

Measure Length

Find Length with a Ruler

1. Look at this section of a ruler. Each centimeter is divided into 10 millimeters. How long is the paper clip?
2. The length of the paper clip is 3 centimeters plus 2 millimeters. You can write this length as 3.2 centimeters.
3. Place a ruler on your desk. Lay a pencil against the ruler so that one end of the pencil lines up with the left edge of the ruler. Record the length of the pencil.
4. Trade pencils with a classmate. Measure and record the length of each other's pencils. Compare your answers.

Measuring Area

Area is the amount of surface something covers. To find the area of a rectangle, multiply the rectangle's length by its width. For example, the rectangle here is 3 centimeters long and 2 centimeters wide. Its area is 3 cm x 2 cm = 6 square centimeters. You write the area as 6 cm^2.

1. Find the area of your science book. Measure the book's length to the nearest centimeter. Measure its width.
2. Multiply the book's length by its width. Remember to put the answer in cm^2.

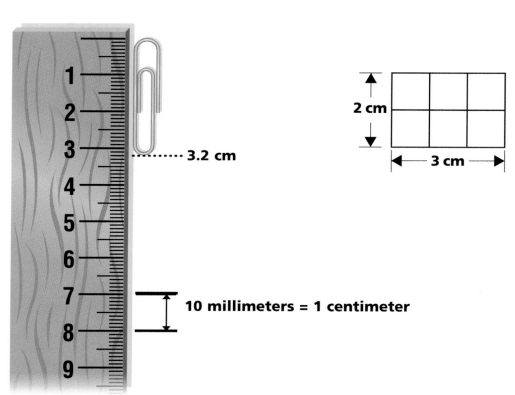

3.2 cm

10 millimeters = 1 centimeter

2 cm

3 cm

Measure Mass

Mass is the amount of matter an object has. You use a balance to measure mass. To find the mass of an object, you balance it with objects whose masses you know. Let's find the mass of a box of crayons.

Measure the Mass of a Box of Crayons

1. Place the balance on a flat, level surface.
2. Make sure the empty pans are balanced with each other. The pointer should point to the middle mark. If it does not, move the slider a little to the right or left to balance the pans.
3. Gently place a box of crayons on the left pan.
4. Add masses to the right pan until the pans are balanced.

5. Count the numbers on the masses that are in the right pan. The total is the mass of the box of crayons, in grams. Record this number. After the number, write a *g* for "grams."

More About Mass

What would happen if you replaced the crayons with a pineapple? You may not have enough masses to balance the pineapple. It has a mass of about 1,000 grams. That's the same as 1 kilogram, because *kilo* means "1,000."

Measure Volume

Have you ever used a measuring cup? Measuring cups measure the volume of liquids. Volume is the amount of space something takes up. In science you use special measuring cups called beakers and graduated cylinders. These containers are marked in milliliters (mL).

Measure the Volume of a Liquid

1. Look at the beaker and at the graduated cylinder. The beaker has marks for each 25 mL up to 200 mL. The graduated cylinder has marks for each 1 mL up to 100 mL.

2. The surface of the water in the graduated cylinder curves up at the sides. You measure the volume by reading the height of the water at the flat part. What is the volume of water in the graduated cylinder? How much water is in the beaker?

3. Pour 50 mL of water from a pitcher into a graduated cylinder. The water should be at the 50-mL mark on the graduated cylinder. If you go over the mark, pour a little water back into the pitcher.

4. Pour the 50 mL of water into a beaker.

5. Repeat steps 3 and 4 using 30 mL, 45 mL, and 25 mL of water.

6. Measure the volume of water you have in the beaker. Do you have about the same amount of water as your classmates?

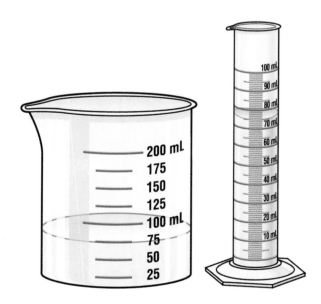

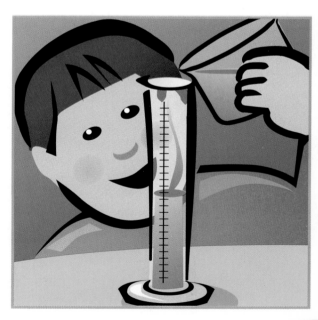

Measure Weight/Force

You use a spring scale to measure weight. An object has weight because the force of gravity pulls down on the object. Therefore, weight is a force. Like all forces, weight is measured in newtons (N).

Measure the Weight of an Object

1. Look at your spring scale to see how many newtons it measures. See how the measurements are divided. The spring scale shown here measures up to 10 N. It has a mark for every 1 N.

2. Hold the spring scale by the top loop. Put the object to be measured on the bottom hook. If the object will not stay on the hook, place it in a net bag. Then hang the bag from the hook.

3. Let go of the object slowly. It will pull down on a spring inside the scale. The spring is connected to a pointer. The pointer on the spring scale shown here is a small arrow.

4. Wait for the pointer to stop moving. Read the number of newtons next to the pointer. This is the object's weight. The mug in the picture weighs 3 N.

More About Spring Scales

You probably weigh yourself by standing on a bathroom scale. This is a spring scale. The force of your body stretches a spring inside the scale. The dial on the scale is probably marked in pounds—the English unit of weight. One pound is equal to about 4.5 newtons.

Here are some spring scales you may have seen.

Measure Temperature

Temperature is how hot or cold something is. You use a thermometer to measure temperature. A thermometer is made of a thin tube with colored liquid inside. When the liquid gets warmer, it expands and moves up the tube. When the liquid gets cooler, it contracts and moves down the tube. You may have seen most temperatures measured in degrees Fahrenheit (°F). Scientists measure temperature in degrees Celsius (°C).

Read a Thermometer

1. Look at the thermometer shown here. It has two scales—a Fahrenheit scale and a Celsius scale. Every 20 degrees on each scale has a number.

2. What is the temperature shown on the thermometer? At what temperature does water freeze? Give your answers in °F and in °C.

How Is Temperature Measured?

1. Fill a large beaker about one-half full of cool water. Find the temperature of the water by holding a thermometer in the water. Do not let the bulb at the bottom of the thermometer touch the sides or bottom of the beaker.

2. Keep the thermometer in the water until the liquid in the tube stops moving—about a minute. Read and record the temperature on the Celsius scale.

3. Fill another large beaker one-half full of warm water from a faucet. Be careful not to burn yourself by using hot water.

4. Find and record the temperature of the warm water just as you did in steps 1 and 2.

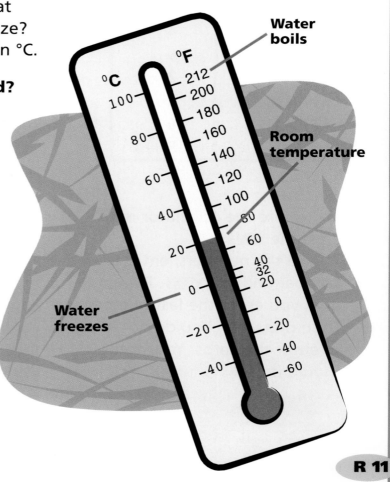

Water boils

Room temperature

Water freezes

°C
100
80
60
40
20
0
-20
-40

°F
212
200
180
160
140
120
100
80
60
40
32
20
0
-20
-40
-60

Use Calculators: Add and Subtract

Sometimes after you make measurements, you have to add or subtract your numbers. A calculator helps you do this.

Add and Subtract Rainfall Amounts

The table shows the amount of rain that fell in a town each week during the summer.

Week	Rain (cm)
1	3
2	5
3	2
4	0
5	1
6	6
7	4
8	0
9	2
10	2
11	6
12	5

1. Make sure the calculator is on. Press the **ON** key.

2. To add the numbers, enter a number and press **+**. Repeat until you enter the last number. Then press **=**. You do not have to enter the zeros. Your total should be 36.

3. What if you found out that you made a mistake in your measurement? Week 1 should be 2 cm less, week 6 should be 3 cm less, week 11 should be 1 cm less, and week 12 should be 2 cm less. Subtract these numbers from your total. You should have 36 displayed on the calculator. Press **−**, and enter the first number you want to subtract. Repeat until you enter the last number. Then press **=**.

Use Calculators: Multiply and Divide

Sometimes after you make measurements, you have to multiply or divide your measurements to get other information. A calculator helps you multiply and divide, especially if the numbers have decimal points.

Multiply Decimals

What if you are measuring the width of your classroom? You discover that the floor is covered with tiles and the room is exactly 32 tiles wide. You measure a tile, and it is 22.7 centimeters wide. To find the width of the room, you can multiply 32 by 22.7.

1. Make sure the calculator is on. Press the **ON** key.
2. Press **3** and **2**.
3. Press **×**.
4. Press **2**, **2**, **·**, and **7**.
5. Press **=**. Your total should be 726.4. That is how wide the room is in centimeters.

Divide Decimals

Now what if you wanted to find out how many desks placed side by side would be needed to reach across the room? You measure one desk, and it is 60 centimeters wide. To find the number of desks needed, divide 726.4 by 60.

1. Turn the calculator on.
2. Press **7**, **2**, **6**, **·**, and **4**.
3. Press **÷**.
4. Press **6** and **0**.
5. Press **=**. Your total should be about 12.1. This means you can fit 12 desks across the room with a little space left over.

What if the room was 35 tiles wide? How wide would the room be? How many desks would fit across it?

Use Computers

A computer has many uses. The Internet connects your computer to many other computers around the world, so you can collect all kinds of information. You can use a computer to show this information and write reports. Best of all, you can use a computer to explore, discover, and learn.

You can also get information from CD-ROMs. They are computer disks that can hold large amounts of information. You can fit a whole encyclopedia on one CD-ROM.

Use Computers for a Project

Here is how one group of students uses computers as they work on a weather project.

1. The students use instruments to measure temperature, wind speed, wind direction, and other parts of the weather. They input this information, or data, into the computer. The students keep the data in a table. This helps them compare the data from one day to the next.

2. The teacher finds out that another group of students in a town 200 kilometers to the west is also doing a weather project. The two groups use the Internet to talk to each other and share data. When a storm happens in the town to the west, that group tells the other group that it's coming its way.

Use Technology

email: It's going to storm here. The sky is turning dark gray. The winds are sometimes 65 km per hour from the northwest.

3. The students want to find out more. They decide to stay on the Internet and send questions to a local TV weather forecaster. She has a website and answers questions from students every day.

4. Meanwhile some students go to the library to gather more information from a CD-ROM disk. The CD-ROM has an encyclopedia that includes movie clips with sound. The clips give examples of different kinds of storms.

5. The students have kept all their information in a folder called Weather Project. Now they use that information to write a report about the weather. On the computer they can move paragraphs, add words, take out words, put in diagrams, and draw their own weather maps. Then they print the report in color.

6. Use the information on these two pages to plan your own investigation. Use a computer, the Internet, a CD-ROM, or any other technological device.

Make Graphs to Organize Data

When you do an experiment in science, you collect information. To find out what your information means, you can organize it into graphs. There are many kinds of graphs.

Bar Graphs

A bar graph uses bars to show information. For example, what if you are growing a plant? Every week you measure how high the plant has grown. Here is what you find.

Week	Height (cm)
1	1
2	3
3	6
4	10
5	17
6	20
7	22
8	23

The bar graph at right organizes the measurements you collected so that you can easily compare them.

1. Look at the bar for week 2. Put your finger at the top of the bar. Move your finger straight over to the left to find how many centimeters the plant grew by the end of week 2.
2. Between which two weeks did the plant grow most?
3. When did plant growth begin to level off?

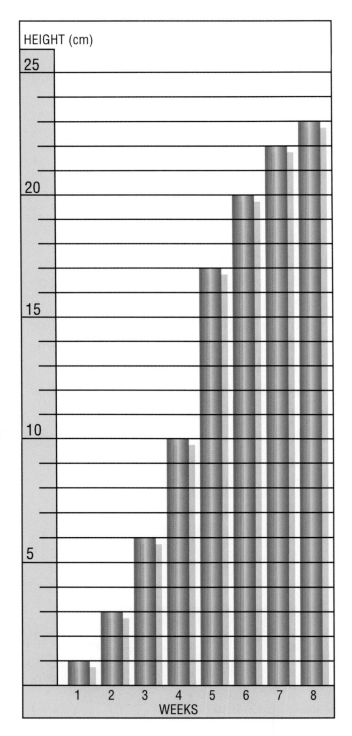

Represent Data

Pictographs

A pictograph uses symbols, or pictures, to show information. What if you collect information about how much water your family uses each day? Here is what you find.

Activity	Water Used Each Day (L)
Drinking	10
Showering	100
Bathing	120
Brushing teeth	40
Washing dishes	80
Washing hands	30
Washing clothes	160
Flushing toilet	50

You can organize this information into the pictograph shown here. In this pictograph each bottle means 20 liters of water. A half bottle means half of 20, or 10 liters of water.

1. Which activity uses the most water?
2. Which activity uses the least water?

Line Graphs

A line graph shows information by connecting dots plotted on the graph. It shows change over time. What if you measure the temperature outdoors every hour starting at 6 A.M.? Here is what you find.

Time	Temperature (°C)
6 A.M.	10
7 A.M.	12
8 A.M.	14
9 A.M.	16
10 A.M.	18
11 A.M.	20

You can organize this information into a line graph. Follow these steps.

1. Make a scale along the bottom and side of the graph. The scales should include all the numbers in the chart. Label the scales.
2. Plot points on the graph.
3. Connect the points with a line.

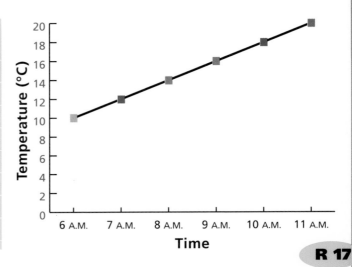

A Family's Daily Use of Water

Drinking	20 liters = of water
Showering	
Bathing	
Brushing teeth	
Washing dishes	
Washing hands	
Washing clothes	
Flushing toilet	

Represent Data

Make Maps, Tables, Charts

Locate Places

A map is a drawing that shows an area from above. Most maps have numbers and letters along the top and side. What if you wanted to find the library on the map below? It is located at D7. Place a finger on the letter D along the side of the map and another finger on the number 7 at the top. Then move your fingers straight across and down the map until they meet. The library is located where D and 7 meet.

1. What building is located at G3?
2. The hospital is located three blocks south and three blocks east of the library. What is its number and letter?
3. Make a map of an area in your community. It might be a park or the area between your home and school. Include numbers and letters along the top and side. Use a compass to find north, and mark north on your map. Exchange maps with classmates.

Idea Maps

The map below left shows how places are connected to each other. Idea maps, on the other hand, show how ideas are connected to each other. Idea maps help you organize information about a topic.

Look at the idea map below. It connects ideas about water. This map shows that Earth's water is either fresh water or salt water. The map also shows four sources of fresh water. You can see that there is no connection between "rivers" and "salt water" on the map. This reminds you that salt water does not flow in rivers.

Make an idea map about a topic you are learning in science. Your map can include words, phrases, or even sentences. Arrange your map in a way that makes sense to you and helps you understand the ideas.

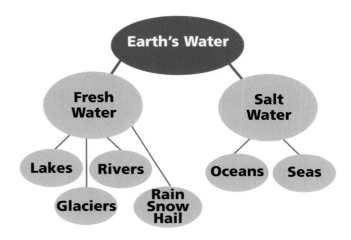

Make Tables and Charts to Organize Data

Tables help to organize data during experiments. Most tables have columns that run up and down, and rows that run across. The columns and rows have headings that tell you what kind of data goes in each part of the table.

A Sample Table

What if you are going to do an experiment to find out how long different kinds of seeds take to sprout? Before you begin the experiment, you should set up your table. Follow these steps.

1. In this experiment you will plant 20 radish seeds, 20 bean seeds, and 20 corn seeds. Your table must show how many of each kind of seed sprouted on days 1, 2, 3, 4, and 5.

2. Make your table with columns, rows, and headings. You might use a computer. Some computer programs let you build a table with just the click of a mouse. You can delete or add columns and rows if you need to.

3. Give your table a title. Your table could look like the one here.

Make a Table

Plant 20 bean seeds in each of two trays. Keep each tray at a different temperature, as shown above, and observe the trays for seven days. Make a table that you can use for this experiment. You can use the table to record, examine, and evaluate the information of this experiment.

Make a Chart

A chart is simply a table with pictures, as well as words to label the rows or columns. Make a chart that shows the information of the above experiment.

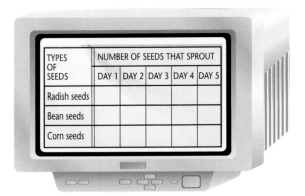

TYPES OF SEEDS	NUMBER OF SEEDS THAT SPROUT				
	DAY 1	DAY 2	DAY 3	DAY 4	DAY 5
Radish seeds					
Bean seeds					
Corn seeds					

The Skeletal System

The body has a supporting frame, called a skeleton, which is made up of bones. The skeleton has several jobs.

- It gives the body its shape.
- It protects organs in the body.
- It works with muscles to move the body.

Each of the 206 bones of the skeleton is the size and shape best fitted to do its job. For example, long and strong leg bones support the body's weight.

The Skeleton

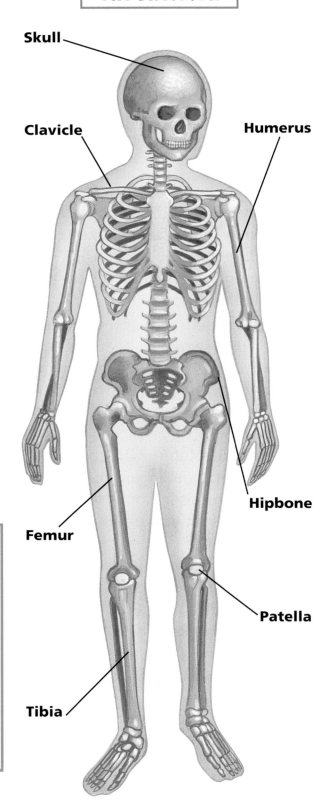

Skull

Clavicle

Humerus

Hipbone

Femur

Patella

Tibia

CARE!

- Exercise to keep your skeletal system in good shape.
- Don't overextend your joints.
- Eat foods rich in vitamins and minerals. Your bones need the minerals calcium and phosphorus to grow strong.

Bones

1 A bone is covered with a tough but thin membrane that has many small blood vessels. The blood vessels bring nutrients and oxygen to the living parts of the bone and remove wastes.

2 Inside some bones is a soft tissue known as marrow. Yellow marrow is made mostly of fat cells and is one of the body's energy reserves. It is usually found in the long, hollow spaces of long bones.

3 Part of the bone is compact, or solid. It is made up of living bone cells and non-living materials. The nonliving part is made up of layers of hardened minerals such as calcium and phosphorus. In between the mineral layers are living bone cells.

4 Red marrow fills the spaces in spongy bone. Red marrow makes new red blood cells, germ-fighting white blood cells, and cell fragments that stop a cut from bleeding.

5 Part of the bone is made of bone tissue that looks like a dry sponge. It is made of strong, hard tubes. It is also found in the middle of short, flat bones.

CARE!

- **Eat foods rich in vitamins and minerals. Your bones need the minerals calcium and phosphorus to grow strong.**
- **Be careful! Avoid sprains and fractures.**
- **Get help in case of injury.**

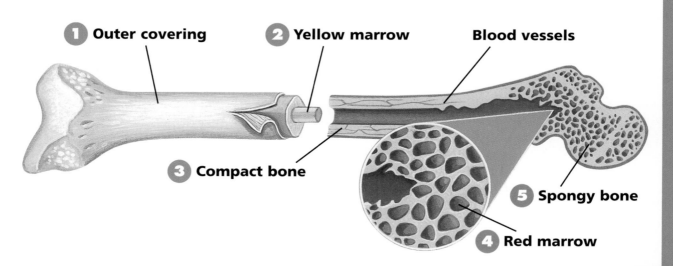

1 Outer covering **2** Yellow marrow Blood vessels **3** Compact bone **5** Spongy bone **4** Red marrow

Joints

The skeleton has different types of joints. A joint is a place where two or more bones meet. Joints can be classified into three major groups—immovable joints, partly movable joints, and movable joints.

Types of Joints

IMMOVABLE JOINTS

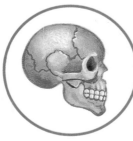

Head

Immovable joints are places where bones fit together too tightly to move. Nearly all the 29 bones in the skull meet at immovable joints. Only the lower jaw can move.

PARTLY MOVABLE JOINTS

Partly movable joints are places where bones can move only a little. Ribs are connected to the breastbone with these joints.

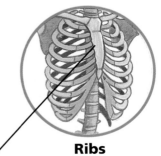

Breastbone

Ribs

MOVABLE JOINTS

Movable joints are places where bones can move easily.

Gliding joint

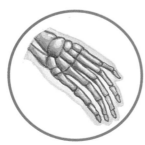

Hand and wrist

Small bones in the wrists and ankles meet at gliding joints. The bones can slide against one another. These joints allow some movement in all directions.

The hips are examples of ball-and-socket joints. The ball of one bone fits into the socket, or cup, of another bone. These joints allow bones to move back and forth, in a circle, and side to side.

Ball-and-socket joint

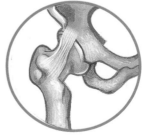

Hip

Hinge joint

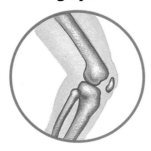

Knee

The knees are hinge joints. A hinge joint is similar to a door hinge. It allows bones to move back and forth in one direction.

The joint between the skull and neck is a pivot joint. It allows the head to move up and down, and side to side.

Pivot joint

Neck

The Muscular System

1 A message from your brain causes this muscle, called the biceps, to contract. When a muscle contracts, it becomes shorter and thicker. As the biceps contracts, it pulls on the arm bone it is attached to.

2 Most muscles work in pairs to move bones. This muscle, called the triceps, relaxes when the biceps contracts. When a muscle relaxes, it becomes longer and thinner.

3 To straighten your arm, a message from your brain causes the triceps to contract. When the triceps contracts, it pulls on the bone it is attached to.

4 As the triceps contracts, the biceps relaxes. Your arm straightens.

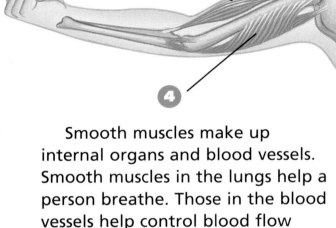

Three types of muscles make up the body—skeletal muscle, cardiac muscle, and smooth muscle.

The muscles that are attached to and move bones are called skeletal muscles. These muscles are attached to bones by a tough cord called a tendon. Skeletal muscles pull bones to move them. Muscles do not push bones.

Cardiac muscles are found in only one place in the body—the heart. The walls of the heart are made of strong cardiac muscles. When cardiac muscles contract, they squeeze blood out of the heart. When cardiac muscles relax, the heart fills with more blood.

Smooth muscles make up internal organs and blood vessels. Smooth muscles in the lungs help a person breathe. Those in the blood vessels help control blood flow around the body.

CARE!

- **Exercise to strengthen your muscles.**
- **Eat the right foods.**
- **Get plenty of rest.**

The Circulatory System

The circulatory system consists of the heart, blood vessels, and blood. Circulation is the flow of blood through the body. Blood is a liquid that contains red blood cells, white blood cells, and platelets. Red blood cells carry oxygen and nutrients to cells. White blood cells work to fight germs that enter the body. Platelets are cell fragments that make the blood clot.

The heart is a muscular organ about the size of a fist. It beats about 70 to 90 times a minute, pumping blood through the blood vessels. Arteries carry blood away from the heart. Some arteries carry blood to the lungs, where the cells pick up oxygen. Other arteries carry oxygen-rich blood from the lungs to all other parts of the body. Veins carry blood from other parts of the body back to the heart. Blood in most veins carries the wastes released by cells and has little oxygen. Blood flows from arteries to veins through narrow vessels called capillaries.

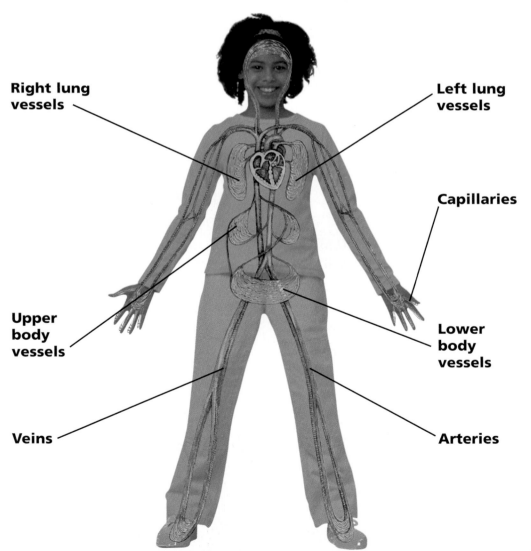

Right lung vessels

Left lung vessels

Capillaries

Upper body vessels

Lower body vessels

Veins

Arteries

The Heart

The heart has two sides, right and left, separated by a thick muscular wall. Each side has two chambers for blood. The upper chamber is the atrium. The lower chamber is the ventricle. Blood enters the heart through the vena cava. It leaves the heart through the aorta.

The pulmonary artery carries blood from the body into the lungs. Here carbon dioxide leaves the blood to be exhaled by the lungs. Fresh oxygen enters the blood to be carried to every cell in the body. Blood returns from the lungs to the heart through the pulmonary veins.

CARE!

- Don't smoke. The nicotine in tobacco makes the heart beat faster and work harder to pump blood.

- Never take illegal drugs, such as cocaine or heroin. They can damage the heart and cause heart failure.

How the Heart Works

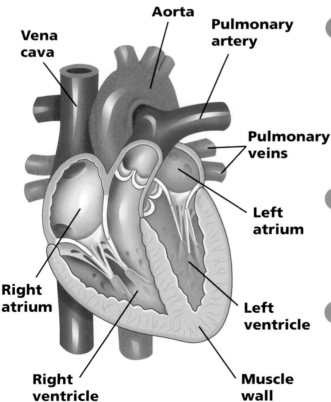

Vena cava

Aorta

Pulmonary artery

Pulmonary veins

Left atrium

Left ventricle

Muscle wall

Right atrium

Right ventricle

To the Lungs

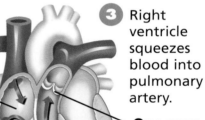

1 The right atrium fills.

Right atrium

2 Right atrium squeezes blood into right ventricle.

3 Right ventricle squeezes blood into pulmonary artery.

One-way valve

Right ventricle

From the Lungs

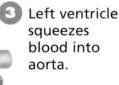

1 The left atrium fills.

2 Left atrium squeezes blood into left ventricle.

3 Left ventricle squeezes blood into aorta.

Left atrium

One-way valve

Left ventricle

The Respiratory System

The process of getting and using oxygen in the body is called respiration. When a person inhales, air is pulled into the nose or mouth. The air travels down into the trachea. In the chest the trachea divides into two bronchial tubes. One bronchial tube enters each lung. Each bronchial tube branches into smaller tubes called bronchioles.

At the end of each bronchiole are tiny air sacs called alveoli. The alveoli exchange carbon dioxide for oxygen.

Oxygen comes from the air we breathe. Two muscles control breathing, the lungs and a dome-shaped sheet of muscle called the diaphragm.

To inhale, the diaphragm contracts and pulls down. To exhale, the diaphragm relaxes and returns to its dome shape.

CARE!

- **Don't smoke. Smoking damages your respiratory system.**

- **Exercise to strengthen your breathing muscles.**

- **If you ever have trouble breathing, tell an adult at once.**

Air Flow

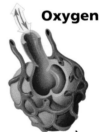

Carbon dioxide | Oxygen

Carbon dioxide diffuses into the alveoli. From there it is exhaled.

Capillary net

Throat

Trachea

Alveoli

Fresh oxygen diffuses from the alveoli to the blood.

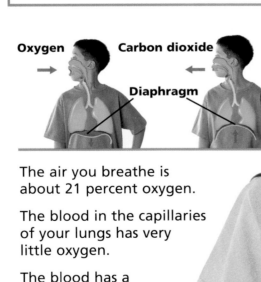

Oxygen →   Carbon dioxide ←

Diaphragm

The air you breathe is about 21 percent oxygen.

The blood in the capillaries of your lungs has very little oxygen.

The blood has a higher concentration of carbon dioxide than air.

Lungs

Activity Pyramid

Physical fitness is the condition in which the body is healthy and works the best it can. It involves working the skeletal muscles, bones, joints, heart, and respiratory system.

Occasionally
Inactive pastimes such as watching TV, playing board games, talking on the phone

2–3 times a week
Leisure activities such as gardening, golf, softball

3–5 times a week
Aerobic activities such as swimming, biking, climbing; sports activities such as basketball, handball

The activity pyramid shows you the kinds of exercises and other activities you should be doing to make your body more physically fit.

Daily Substitute activity for inactivity—take the stairs, walk instead of riding, bike instead of taking the bus

Food Guide Pyramid

To make sure the body stays fit and healthy, a person needs to eat a balanced diet. The Food Guide Pyramid shows how many servings of each group a person should eat every day.

CARE!

- **Stay active every day.**
- **Eat a balanced diet.**
- **Drink plenty of water— 6 to 8 large glasses a day.**

Fats, oils, and sweets
Use sparingly

Milk, yogurt, and cheese group
2–3 servings

Meat, dry beans, eggs, and nuts group
2–3 servings

Vegetable group
3–5 servings

Fruit group
2–4 servings

Bread, cereal, rice, and pasta group
6–11 servings

The Digestive System

Digestion is the process of breaking down food into simple substances the body can use. Digestion begins when a person chews food. Chewing breaks the food down into smaller pieces and moistens it with saliva. Saliva is produced by the salivary glands.

Digested food is absorbed in the small intestine. The walls of the small intestine are lined with villi. Villi are tiny fingerlike projections that absorb digested food. From the villi the blood transports nutrients to every part of the body.

CARE!

- Chew your food well.
- Drink plenty of water to help move food through your digestive system.

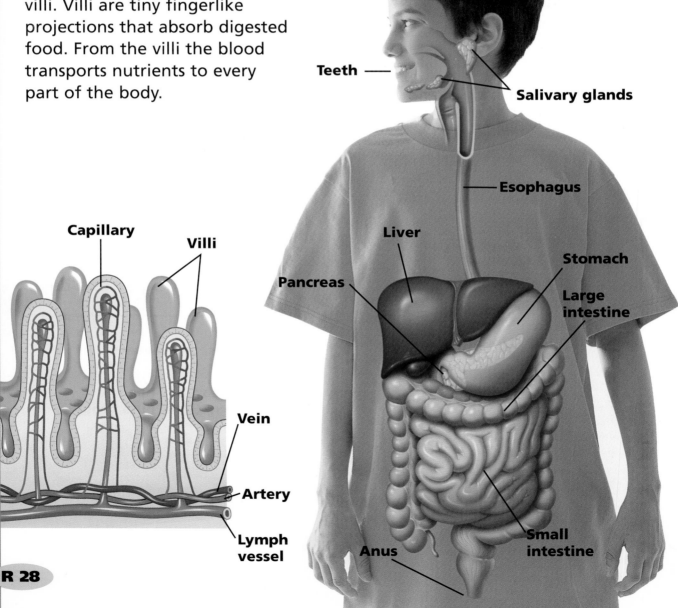

Capillary

Villi

Vein

Artery

Lymph vessel

Teeth

Salivary glands

Esophagus

Liver

Pancreas

Stomach

Large intestine

Small intestine

Anus

The Excretory System

Excretion is the process of removing waste products from the body. The liver filters wastes from the blood and converts them into urea. Urea is then carried to the kidneys for excretion.

The skin takes part in excretion when a person sweats. Glands in the inner layer of the skin produce sweat. Sweat is mostly water. Sweat tastes salty because it contains mineral salts the body doesn't need. There is also a tiny amount of urea in sweat.

Sweat is excreted onto the outer layer of the skin. Evaporation into the air takes place in part because of body heat. When sweat evaporates, a person feels cooler.

How You Sweat

Glands under your skin push sweat up to the surface, where it collects.

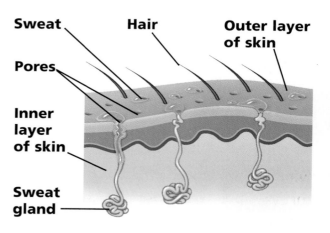

Sweat, Hair, Outer layer of skin, Pores, Inner layer of skin, Sweat gland

CARE!

- **Wash regularly to avoid body odor, clogged pores, and skin irritation.**

How Your Kidneys Work

1 Blood enters the kidney through an artery and flows into capillaries.

2 Sugars, salts, water, urea, and other wastes move from the capillaries to tiny nephrons.

3 Nutrients return to the blood and flow back out through veins.

4 Urea and other wastes become urine, which flows down the ureters.

5 Urine is stored in the bladder and excreted through the urethra.

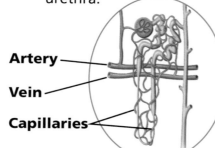

Artery, Vein, Capillaries

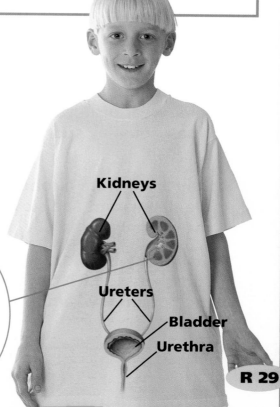

Kidneys, Ureters, Bladder, Urethra

The Nervous System

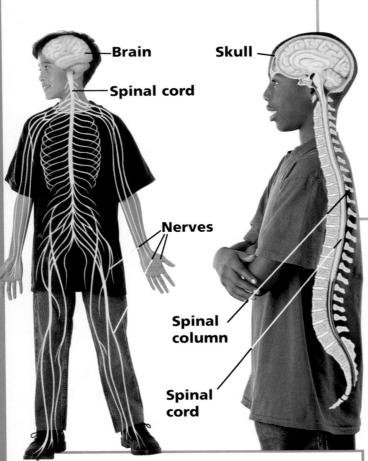

Brain
Spinal cord

Skull

Nerves

Spinal column

Spinal cord

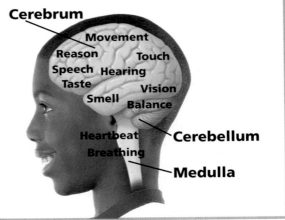

Cerebrum
Movement
Reason
Touch
Speech
Hearing
Taste
Vision
Smell
Balance
Heartbeat
Breathing
Cerebellum
Medulla

CARE!

- To protect the brain and spinal cord, wear protective headgear when you play sports or exercise.

- Stay away from alcohol, which is a depressant and slows down the nervous system.

- Stay away from drugs, such as stimulants, which can speed up the nervous system.

The nervous system has two parts. The brain and the spinal cord are the central nervous system. All other nerves are the outer nervous system.

The largest part of the brain is the cerebrum. A deep groove separates the right half, or hemisphere, of the cerebrum from the left half. Both sides of the cerebrum contain control centers for the senses.

The cerebellum lies below the cerebrum. It coordinates the skeletal muscles. It also helps in keeping balance.

The brain stem connects to the spinal cord. The lowest part of the brain stem is the medulla. It controls heartbeat, breathing, blood pressure, and the muscles in the digestive system.

The Endocrine System

Hormones are chemicals that control body functions. A gland that produces hormones is called an endocrine gland. Sweat from sweat glands flows out of tubes called ducts. Endocrine glands have no ducts.

The endocrine glands are scattered around the body. Each gland makes one or more hormones. Every hormone seeks out a target organ. This is the place in the body where the hormone acts.

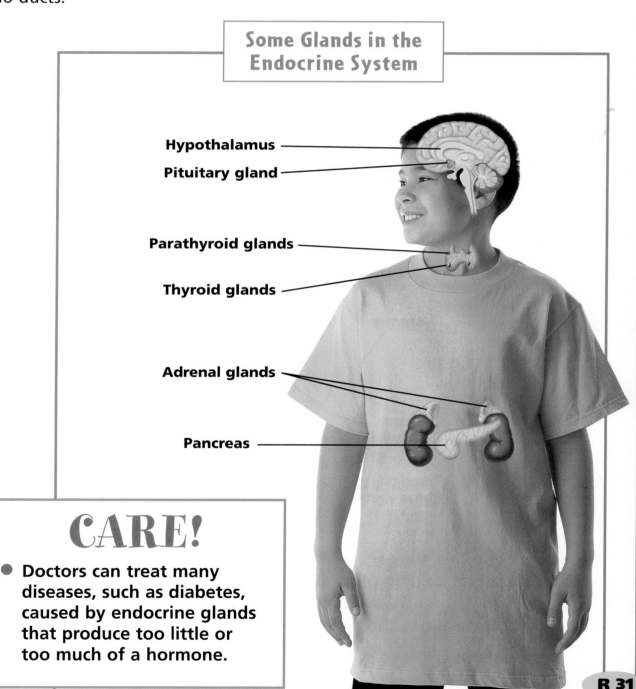

Some Glands in the Endocrine System

- Hypothalamus
- Pituitary gland
- Parathyroid glands
- Thyroid glands
- Adrenal glands
- Pancreas

CARE!

- Doctors can treat many diseases, such as diabetes, caused by endocrine glands that produce too little or too much of a hormone.

The Senses

Seeing

Retina **Cornea**

Optic nerve **Iris** **Lens**

Light reflected from an object enters the eye and falls on the retina. Receptor cells change the light into electrical signals, or impulses. These impulses travel along the optic nerve to the vision center of the brain.

1 Light reflects off the tree and into your eyes.

2 The light passes through your cornea and the pupil in your iris.

3 Your eye bends the light so it hits your retina.

4 Receptor cells on your retina change the light into electrical signals.

5 The impulses travel along neurons in your optic nerve to the seeing center of your brain.

Hearing

1 Your outer ear collects sound waves.

Hammer

Auditory nerve

Hearing center

7 The impulses travel along your auditory nerve to the brain's hearing center.

2 They are funneled down your ear canal.

Eardrum

Anvil

6 Receptor cells inside your cochlea change.

Cochlea

3 The eardrum vibrates.

4 Three tiny ear bones vibrate.

Stirrup

5 The cochlea vibrates.

Sound waves enter the ear and cause the eardrum to vibrate. Receptor cells in the ear change the sound waves into impulses that travel along the auditory nerve to the hearing center of the brain.

CARE!

- Avoid loud music.
- Don't sit too close to the TV screen.

The Senses

Smelling

The sense of smell is really the ability to detect chemicals in the air. When a person breathes, chemicals dissolve in mucus in the upper part of the nose. When the chemicals come in contact with receptor cells, the cells send impulses along the olfactory nerve to the smelling center of the brain.

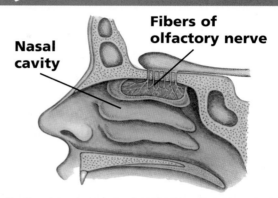

Nasal cavity

Fibers of olfactory nerve

Tasting

When a person eats, chemicals in food dissolve in saliva. Inside each taste bud are receptors that can sense the four main tastes—sweet, sour, salty, and bitter. The receptors send impulses along a nerve to the taste center of the brain. The brain identifies the taste of the food.

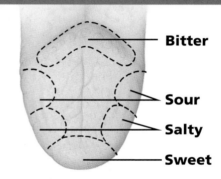

Bitter

Sour

Salty

Sweet

Touching

Receptor cells in the skin help a person tell hot from cold, wet from dry, and the light touch of a feather from the pressure of stepping on a stone. Each receptor cell sends impulses along sensory nerves to the spinal cord. The spinal cord then sends the impulses to the touch center of the brain.

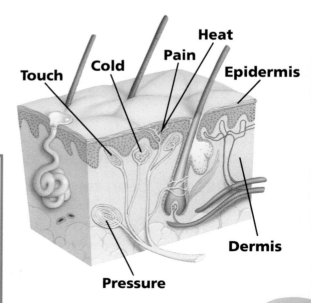

Touch

Cold

Pain

Heat

Epidermis

Dermis

Pressure

CARE!

- **To prevent the spread of germs, always cover your mouth and nose when you cough or sneeze.**

The Immune System

The immune system helps the body fight disease. When a person has a cut, germ-fighting white blood cells rush to the wound. There are white blood cells in the blood vessels and in the lymph vessels. Lymph vessels are similar to blood vessels. Instead of blood, they carry lymph. Lymph is a straw-colored fluid surrounding body cells.

Lymph nodes filter out harmful materials in the body. They also produce white blood cells to fight infections. Swollen lymph nodes in the neck are a clue that the body is fighting germs.

Lymph vessels run through your body to collect fluid and return it to the bloodstream.

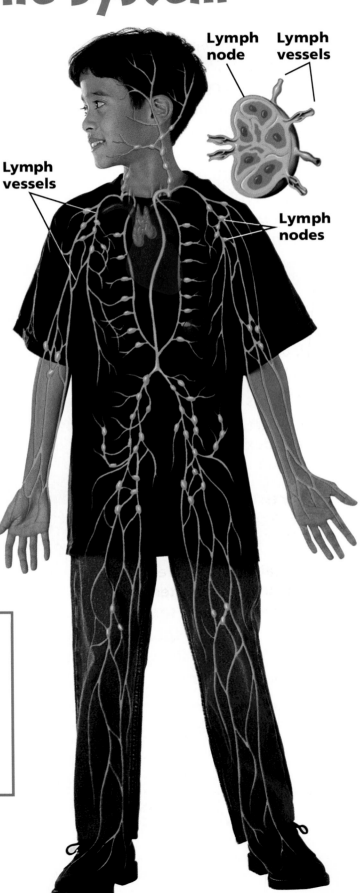

Lymph node   Lymph vessels

Lymph vessels

Lymph nodes

CARE!

- Be sure to get immunized against common diseases.
- Keep cuts clean to prevent infection.

Glossary

This Glossary will help you to pronounce and understand the meanings of the Science Words introduced in this book. The page number at the end of the definition tells where the word appears.

A

acceleration (ak sel′ə rā′shən) Any change in the speed or direction of a moving object. (p. F8)

acid rain (as′id rān) Harmful moisture that falls to Earth after being mixed with wastes from burned fossil fuels. (p. A59)

adaptation (a′dap′tā′shən) A special trait that helps an organism survive. (p. B66)

air mass (âr mas) A large region of the atmosphere where the air has similar properties throughout. (p. D79)

air pressure (âr presh′ər) The force put on a given area by the weight of the air above it. (p. D67)

alloy (al′oi) A mixture of two or more elements, very often of metals. (p. E38)

alternating current (ôl′tər nā ting kûr′ənt) Current that flows in a circuit, first in one direction, then in the opposite direction. (p. F94)

amber (am′bər) Hardened tree sap, yellow to brown in color, often a source of insect fossils. (p. C20)

ampere (am′pîr) The unit used to measure the number of electrical charges that flow past a certain point in one second. (p. F79)

amphibian (am fib′ē ən) A cold-blooded vertebrate that spends part of its life in water and part of its life on land. (p. B31)

amplitude (am′pli tüd′) The energy in a sound wave. (p. F59)

anther (an′thər) The part of the plant that produces the pollen. (p. A84)

area (âr′ē ə) The number of unit squares that fit inside a surface. (p. E17)

PRONUNCIATION KEY

The following symbols are used throughout the McGraw-Hill Science 2002 Glossaries.

a	at	e	end	o	hot	u	up	hw	white	ə	about
ā	ape	ē	me	ō	old	ū	use	ng	song		taken
ä	far	i	it	ôr	fork	ü	rule	th	thin		pencil
âr	care	ī	ice	oi	oil	ù	pull	th	this		lemon
ô	law	îr	pierce	ou	out	ûr	turn	zh	measure		circus

′ = primary accent; shows which syllable takes the main stress, such as **kil** in **kilogram** (kil′ə gram′).

′ = secondary accent; shows which syllables take lighter stresses, such as **gram** in **kilogram**.

arthropod (är'thrə pod') An invertebrate with jointed legs and a body that is divided into sections. (p. B21)

asteroid (as'tə roid') Chunks of rock and metal that orbit the Sun. (p. C86)

atmosphere (at'məs fîr') The blanket of gases that surrounds Earth. (p. D6)

atom (at'əm) The smallest particle of an element. Atoms of one element are all alike but are different from those of any other element. (p. E32)

axis (ak'sis) A real or imaginary line that a spinning object turns around. (p. C67)

B

bacteria (bak tîr'ē ə) *pl. n., sing.* **bacterium** (-ē əm) One-celled organisms that have cell walls but no nuclei. (p. A13)

balance (bal'əns) An instrument used to measure mass. (p. E8)

basalt (bə sôlt') A fine-grained volcanic rock. (p. C9)

budding (bud'ing) A form of reproduction in simple invertebrates where a bud forms on the adult's body and slowly develops into a new organism before breaking off. (p. B60)

buoyancy (boi'ən sē) The upward force of water, another liquid, or air that keeps things afloat. (p. E7)

C

camouflage (kam'ə fläzh') An adaptation by which an animal can hide by blending in with its surroundings. (p. B66)

carnivore (kär'nə vôr') A consumer that eats only animals. (p. A48)

cast (kast) A fossil formed or shaped within a mold. (p. C19)

cell (sel) The smallest unit of living matter. (p. A7)

cell membrane (sel mem'brān) A thin outer covering of a cell. (p. A9)

chemical change (kəm'i kəl chānj) A change that produces new matter with different properties from the original matter. *See* **physical change**. (p. E52)

chlorophyll (klôr'ə fil') A green substance in plant cells that helps plants make food by trapping the Sun's energy. (pp. A7, A73)

chromosome (krō'mə sōm') One of the threadlike structures inside a cell's nucleus that control an organism's traits. (p. A9)

circuit (sûr'kit) A complete path through which electricity can flow. (p. F78)

circuit breaker (sûr'kit brā'kər) A reusable switch that protects circuits from dangerously high currents. (p. F84)

circulatory system (sûr′kyə lə tôr′ē sis′təm) The organ system that moves blood through the body. (p. B46)

cirrus cloud (sir′əs kloud) A high-altitude cloud with a featherlike shape, made of ice crystals. (p. D71)

class (klas) A smaller group within a phlyum, such as all those animals that produce milk for their young. Classes are made up of smaller groups called orders. (p. A22)

classify (klas′ə fī) To place things that share properties together in groups. (p. S7)

clone (klōn) An exact copy of its parent formed during reproduction. (p. B60)

cloud (kloud) A mass of tiny droplets of condensed water in the atmosphere. (p. D17)

cnidarian (nī dâr′ē ən) An invertebrate with poison stingers on tentacles. (p. B17)

cold front (kōld frunt) A front where cold air moves in under a warm air mass. (p. D81)

cold-blooded (kōld′blud′id) Said of an animal that cannot control its body temperature. (p. B28)

comet (kom′it) A chunk of ice and rock that orbits the Sun in a long, narrow orbit. (p. C86)

communicate (kə mū′ni kāt′) To share information. (p. S7)

community (kə mū′ni tē) The living part of an ecosystem. (p. A40)

compound (kom′pound) A substance made when two or more elements are joined together and lose their own properties. (p. E36)

compound machine (kom′pound mə shēn′) A combination of two or more simple machines. (p. F29)

concave lens (kän kāv′ lenz) A lens that is thinner in the middle than at the edges, spreading light rays apart and making images appear smaller. (p. F47)

condensation (kon′den sa′shən) The process in which water particles change from a gas to a liquid. (p. D17)

conduction (kən duk′shən) The transfer of energy between two objects that are touching. (p. F36)

conductor (kən duk′tər) A material through which heat or electricity flows easily. (pp. F34, F72)

PRONUNCIATION KEY

a at; ā ape; ä far; âr care; ô law; e end; ē me; i it; ī ice; îr pierce; o hot; ō old; ôr fork; oi oil; ou out; u up; ū use; ü rule; ù pull; ûr turn; hw white; ng song; th thin; <u>th</u> this; zh measure; ə about, taken, pencil, lemon, circus

constellation (kon′stə lā′shən) A number of stars that appears to form a pattern. (p. C88)

consumer (kən sü′mər) Any organism that eats the food producers make or eats other consumers. (p. A46)

contract (*v.*, kən trakt′) To shrink or decrease in size, as most matter does when it cools. (p. F37)

convection (kən′vek′shən) The transfer of energy by the flow of liquids or gases, such as water boiling in a pot or warm air rising in a room. (p. F36)

convex lens (kän veks′ lenz) A lens that bulges in the middle, bringing rays of light together and making images appear larger. (p. F46)

cornea (kôr′nē ə) The thin, clear tissue covering the eye. (p. F48)

crater (krā′tər) A hollow area or pit in the ground. (p. C71)

crest (krest) The highest part of a wave. (p. D32)

crust (krust) Solid rock that makes up the Moon's and Earth's outermost layers. (p. C58)

cumulus cloud (kū′myə ləs kloud) A puffy cloud that appears to rise up from a flat bottom. (p. D71)

current (kûr′ənt) An ocean movement; a large stream of water that flows in the ocean. (p. D28)

current electricity (kûr′ənt i lek tris′i tē) A moving electrical charge. (p. F78)

cytoplasm (sī′tə pla′zəm) A jellylike substance that fills a cell. (p. A9)

D

decomposer (dē′kəm pōz′ər) An organism that breaks down wastes and the remains of other organisms. (p. A46)

deep ocean current (dēp ō′shən kûr′ənt) A stream of water that flows more than 650 feet (200 meters) beneath the sea. (p. D28)

define terms based on observations (di fīn′ tûrms bāst ôn ob′zər vā′shənz) To put together a description that relies on examination and experience. (p. S7)

density (den′si tē) The amount of matter in a given space. In scientific terms, density is the mass per unit of volume. (p. E20)

deposition (dep′ə zish′ən) The dropping off of soil and rock particles by waves, wind, running water, or glaciers. *See* **erosion**. (p. D34)

digestive system (di jes′tiv sis′təm) The organ system that breaks down food for fuel. (p. B49)

direct current (di rekt′ kûr′ənt) Current that flows in one direction through a circuit. (p. F94)

discharge (*n.*, dis'chärj; *v.*, dis chärj') The sudden movement of an electric charge from the object where it built up onto another nearby object. (p. F72)

drought (drout) A long period of time with little or no precipitation. (pp. A56, D42)

drumlin (drum'lin) An oval mound of glacial till. (p. C35)

dry cell (drī sel) A battery that changes chemical energy into electrical energy. It is made of a carbon rod and a moist chemical paste. (p. F81)

E

earthquake (ûrth'kwāk) Movement or vibration in the rocks that make up Earth's crust. (p. C54)

echinoderm (i ki'nə dûrm') A spiny-skinned invertebrate. (p. B20)

ecology (ē kol'ə jē) The study of how living and nonliving things interact. (p. A40)

ecosystem (ek'ō sis'təm) The living and nonliving things in an environment and all their interactions. (p. A40)

efficiency (i fish'ən sē) The measure of how much useful work a machine puts out compared to the amount of work put into it. (p. F30)

effort force (ef'ərt fôrs) The amount of force needed to move something. (p. F22)

egg (eg) The female sex cell. (p. B61)

electric motor (i lek'trik mō'tər) A power source that transforms electrical energy into movement, or mechanical energy. (p. F93)

electrode (i lek'trōd) The negative or positive terminal of a wet cell. The positive electrode is made of copper, the negative electrode of zinc. (p. F81)

electromagnet (i lek'trō mag'nit) A temporary magnet created when current flows through wire wrapped in coils around an iron bar. (p. F92)

electromagnetic spectrum (i lek'trō mag net'ik spek'trəm) A range of all waves of varying wavelengths, including the visible spectrum. It ranges from radio waves, the longest waves with the lowest energy, to gamma waves, the shortest waves with the highest energy. (p. F43)

PRONUNCIATION KEY

a at; ā ape; ä far; âr care; ô law; e end; ē me; i it; ī ice; îr pierce; o hot; ō old; ôr fork; oi oil; ou out; u up; ū use; ü rule; ú pull; ûr turn; hw white; ng song; th thin; th this; zh measure; ə about, taken, pencil, lemon, circus

element (el'ə mənt) A substance that is made up of only one type of matter. (p. E32)

embryo (em'brē ō') A developing organism that results from fertilization. (pp. A33, B61)

endoskeleton (en'dō skel'i tən) An internal supporting structure. (p. B20)

energy (en'ər jē) The ability to do work, either to make an object move or to change matter. (p. F14)

epidermis (e'pə dûr'mis) The outermost protective layer of a leaf. (p. A73)

erosion (i rō'zhən) The wearing away of soil and rock particles by waves, wind, running water, or glaciers. *See* **deposition**. (p. D34)

erratic (i rat'ik) An isolated boulder left behind by a glacier. (p. C37)

evaporation (i vap'ə rā'shən') The process in which water particles change from a liquid to a gas. (pp. D16, E35)

evolution (ev'ə lü'shən) The change in living things over time. (p. A30)

excretory system (ek'skri tōr'ē sis'təm) The organ system that removes liquid wastes. (p. B47)

exoskeleton (ek'sō skel'i tən) A hard covering that protects an invertebrate's body. (p. B21)

expand (ek spand') To increase in size, as most matter does when it is heated. (p. F37)

experiment (ek sper'ə ment') To perform a test to support or disprove a hypothesis. (p. S7)

extinct (ek stingkt') Said of an organism no longer alive on Earth. (p. A33)

family (fam'ə lē) A smaller group of organisms within a class. Families are made up of still smaller groups of very similar organisms called genuses. (p. A22)

fault (fôlt) A break in Earth's outer layer caused by the movement of rocks. (p. C56)

fertilization (fûr'tə lə zā'shən) The joining of a female sex cell, the egg, and a male sex cell, the sperm, to produce a fertilized egg. (pp. A85, B61)

fertilizer (fûr'tə lī'zər) Chemical or animal waste used to treat the soil. (p. D51)

fibrous root (fī'brəs rüt) One of the many hairy branching roots that is one of the two main types of plant roots. *See* **taproot**. (p. A71)

filter (fil'tər) A tool used to separate things by size. It works by means of a mesh or screen that retains the bigger pieces but allows smaller pieces to fall through the holes of the filter. (p. E35)

filtration (fil trā'shən) The passing of a liquid through materials that remove impurities. (p. D52)

food chain (füd chān) The set of steps in which organisms get the food they need to survive. (pp. A48, B7)

food web (füd web) The pattern that shows how food chains are related. (pp. A50, B7)

force (fôrs) Any push or pull that makes an object start moving, stop moving, speed up, slow down, or change direction. (p. F10)

form a hypothesis (fôrm ə hī poth'ə sis) To make a statement that can be tested to answer to a question. (p. S7)

fossil (fos'əl) Any evidence of an organism that lived in the past. (pp. A30, C14)

fossil fuel (fos'əl fū'əl) A substance such as coal or oil that was formed millions of years ago from the remains of plants and animals. These fuels are nonrenewable resources, and when burned for energy, are a major source of pollution. (p. F38)

frame of reference (frāme uv ref'ər əns) A description of the position of an object in terms of other objects that surround it. (p. F6)

freeze (frēz) The process in which moving particles in water slow down, lose heat, and change from a liquid to a solid. (p. D19)

frequency (frē'kwən sē) The number of times a sound source vibrates in one second. (p. F58)

friction (frik'shən) A force between surfaces that slows objects down or stops them from moving. (p. F11)

front (frunt) A boundary between air masses with different temperatures. (p. D80)

fulcrum (fŭl'krəm) A fixed point that supports the bar of a lever and allows the bar to turn, or pivot. (p. F22)

fungi (fun'jī) *pl. n., sing.* **fungus** (fung'gəs) One- or many-celled organisms that absorb food from dead organisms. (p. A13)

fuse (fūz) A device that melts to keep too much electric current from flowing through wires. Once melted, a fuse cannot be reused. (p. F84)

G

gas (gas) A state of matter that does not take up a definite amount of space and has no definite shape. (p. E9)

gears (gîrz) Wheels with teeth that fit together, used for transmitting or changing motion. (p. F28)

PRONUNCIATION KEY

a at; ā ape; ä far; âr care; ô law; e end; ē me; i it; ī ice; îr pierce; o hot; ō old; ôr fork; oi oil; ou out; u up; ū use; ü rule; u̇ pull; ûr turn; hw white; ng song; th thin; <u>th</u> this; zh measure; ə about, taken, pencil, lemon, circus

generator (jen′ər rā′tər) A device that creates alternating current by spinning an electric coil between the poles of a powerful magnet. (p. F94)

genus (jēn′əs) A group made up of two or more very similar species. (p. A25)

germination (jûr′mə nā′shən) The sprouting of a seed into a new plant. (p. A82)

gizzard (giz′ərd) A muscular organ in birds that breaks down food with stored pebbles. (p. B49)

glacial till (glā′shəl til) An unsorted mixture of rock materials deposited as a glacier melts. (p. C35)

glacier (glā′shər) A large mass of snow and ice that slowly moves downward and outward over the land. (pp. C34, D8)

gneiss (nīs) A metamorphic rock composed of alternating light and dark layers. (p. C12)

gram (g) (gram) A unit used to measure the mass of small objects. There are 1,000 *grams* in one *kilogram*. *See* **kilogram**. (p. E8)

grounded (ground′əd) Said of an electric charge that flows into the ground, or surface of Earth. (p. F74)

groundwater (ground′wô′tər) Water stored in the cracks of underground rocks. (p. D10)

H

habitat (hab′i tat′) The home of an organism. (p. A40)

heat (hēt) The movement of thermal energy from warmer to cooler objects. (p. F34)

herbivore (hûr′bə vôr′) A consumer that eats only plants. (p. A48)

heredity (hə red′i tē) The passing of traits from parent to offspring. (p. B62)

horizon (hə rī′zən) A layer of soil differing from the layers above and below it. (p. C45)

humidity (hū mid′i tē) A measurement of how much water vapor is in air. (p. D66)

humus (hū′məs) Leftover decomposed plant and animal matter in the soil. (p. C44)

I

ice cap (īs kap) A thick sheet of ice covering a large area of land. (p. D8)

igneous rock (ig′nē əs rok) "Fire-made" rock formed from melted rock material. (p. C9)

imprint (*n.,* im′print′) A fossil created by a print or an impression. (p. C18)

inclined plane (in klīnd′ plān) A straight, slanted surface, that is not moved when it is used. (p. F26)

inertia (i nûr′shə) The tendency of an object to remain in motion or to stay at rest unless acted upon by an outside force. (p. F11)

infer (in fûr′) To form an idea from facts or observations. (p. S7)

inherited behavior (in her′i təd bi hāv′yər) A behavior that is inborn, not learned. (p. B70)

inner core (in′ər kôr) A sphere of solid material at the center of the Moon or Earth. (p. C58)

instinct (in′stingkt′) A pattern of behavior that requires no thinking because it is programmed into an animal's brain. (p. B70)

insulator (in′sə lā′tər) A material through which heat or electricity does not flow easily. (pp. F34, F72)

interpret data (in tûr′prit dā′tə) To use the information that has been gathered to answer questions or solve a problem. (p. S7)

invertebrate (in vûr′tə brāt′) An animal without a backbone. (p. B8)

irrigation (ir′i gā′shən) A way to get water into the soil by artificial means. (p. D50)

K

kilogram (kg) (kil′ə gram′) The standard unit used to measure mass. *See* **gram**. (p. E8)

kinetic energy (ki net′ik en′ər jē) The energy an object has because it is moving. (p. F14)

kingdom (king′dəm) The largest group into which an organism can be classified. (p. A20)

L

larva (lar′və) A worm-like stage of some organisms that hatches from an egg during complete metamorphosis; a young organism with a form different from its parents. (p. B56)

law of reflection (lô uv ri flek′shən) When light strikes a surface such as a mirror, it is reflected at any outgoing angle equal to its incoming angle. (p. F45)

leaf (lēf) A part of the plant that makes most of the plant's food. (p. A70)

learned behavior (lûrnd bi hāv′yər) Behavior that is not inborn. (p. B71)

PRONUNCIATION KEY

a at; ā ape; ä far; âr care; ô law; e end; ē me; i it; ī ice; îr pierce; o hot; ō old; ôr fork; oi oil; ou out; u up; ū use; ü rule; ù pull; ûr turn; hw white; ng song; th thin; <u>th</u> this; zh measure; ə about, taken, pencil, lemon, circus

length (lengkth) The number of units that fit along one edge of an object. (p. E16)

lever (lev'ər) A simple machine made of a rigid bar or plank and a fixed point, called a fulcrum. (p. F22)

life cycle (līf sī'kəl) The stages of growth and change of an organism's life. (p. B58)

life span (līf span) How long an organism can be expected to live. (p. B59)

lightning (līt'ning) A discharge of static electricty from a thundercloud. (p. F73)

liquid (lik'wid) A state of matter that takes up a definite amount of space but has no definite shape. (p. E9)

load (lōd) The object being lifted or moved by a machine. (p. F22)

luster (lus'tər) The way a mineral reflects light. (p. C7)

M

magnetic field (mag net'ik fēld) A region of magnetic force around a magnet. (p. F91)

make a model (māk ə mod'əl) To make something to represent an object or event. (p. S7)

mammal (mam'əl) A warm-blooded vertebrate with hair or fur; female mammals produce milk to feed their young. (p. B34)

mantle (man'təl) The layer of rock lying below the crust. (p. C58)

mass (mas) The amount of matter making up an object. (p. E8)

matter (ma'tər) Anything that has mass and takes up space. (p. E6)

measure (mezh'ər) To find the size, volume, area, mass, weight, or temperature of an object, or how long an event occurs. (p. S7)

melt (melt) When water particles absorb heat energy and change from a solid to a liquid. (p. D19)

metamorphic rock (mət'ə môr'fik rok) Rock whose form has been changed by heat and/or pressure. (p. C12)

metamorphosis (met'ə môr'fə sis) A process of changes in form during an animal's development. (p. B56)

meteor (mē'tē ər) A fragment of rock, ice, or metal that burns up in Earth's atmosphere. (p. C86)

meteorite (mē'tē ə rīt') A chunk of rock from space that hit Earth. (p. C86)

metric system (met'rik sis'təm) A system of measurement based on units of 10. Metric units such as the meter, kilogram, and liter are used in most countries and in all scientific work. *See* **standard unit.** (p. E16)

microorganism (mī'krō ôr'gə niz'əm) An organism that is so small you need a microscope to see it. (p. A12)

mimicry (mim′i krē) When one organism imitates the traits of another. (p. B68)

mineral (min′ə rəl) A naturally occurring substance, neither a plant nor animal. (p. C6)

mixture (miks′chər) Two or more types of matter that are mixed together but keep their own properties. (p. E34)

mold (mold) A type of fossil that is a hollow form with a particular shape. (p. C18)

mollusk (mol′əsk) A soft-bodied invertebrate. (p. B20)

moraine (mə rān′) Rock debris carried and deposited by a glacier. (p. C35)

muscular system (mus′kyə lər sis′təm) The organ system made up of muscles that move bones. (p. B52)

N

nervous system (nûr′vəs sis′təm) The organ system that controls all other body systems. (p. B50)

neutron star (nü′tron stär) The remnant of a supernova that has become a very dense star. (p. E21)

newton (nü′tən) A metric unit for weight, measuring the pull of gravity between an object and Earth. (p. E19)

nucleus (nü′klē əs) A cell's central control station. (p. A9)

nymph (nimf) A stage of some organisms that hatch from an egg during incomplete metamorphosis; a *nymph* is a young insect that looks like an adult. (p. B57)

O

observe (əb sûrv′) To use one or more of the senses to identify or learn about an object or event. (p. S7)

omnivore (om′nə vôr′) A consumer that eats both plants and animals. (p. A48)

opaque (ō pāk′) Completely blocking light from passing through it. (p. F49)

orbit (ôr′bit) The path an object follows as it revolves. (p. C68)

order (ôr′dər) A smaller group within a class. Orders are made up of still smaller groups of similar organisms called families. (p. A22)

organ (ôr′gən) A group of tissues that work together to do a certain job. (p. A15)

PRONUNCIATION KEY

a at; ā ape; ä far; âr care; ô law; e end; ē me; i it; ī ice; îr pierce; o hot; ō old; ôr fork; oi oil; ou out; u up; ū use; ü rule; u̇ pull; ûr turn; hw white; ng song; th thin; <u>th</u> this; zh measure; ə about, taken, pencil, lemon, circus

organ system (ôr′gən sis′təm) A group of organs that work together to carry on life functions. (p. A15)

organism (ôr′gə niz′əm) A living thing that carries out five basic life functions on its own. (p. A6)

outer core (out′ər kôr) A liquid layer of Earth lying below the mantle. (p. C58)

outwash plain (out′wôsh plān) Gravel, sand, and clay carried from glaciers by melting water and streams. (p. C37)

ovary (ō′və rē) A structure containing egg cells. (p. A85)

overpopulation (ō′vər pop′yə la′shən) A depletion of resources that occurs when too many of at least one kind of living thing inhabits an ecosystem. (p. A57)

oxygen (ok′sə jən) A part of the air that is needed by most plants and animals to live. (p. A6)

P

parallel circuit (par′ə lel′ sûr′kit) A circuit in which each object is connected to the cell separately. (p. F82)

periodic (pîr′ē od′ik) Repeating in a pattern, like the periodic table of the elements. (p. E32)

permeability (pûr′mē ə bil′i tē) The rate at which water can pass through a material. Water passes quickly through porous soils with a high permeability. (p. C49)

petrified (pet′rə fīd′) Said of parts of plants or animals, especially wood and bone, that have been preserved by being "turned to stone." (p. C21)

phase (fāz) One of the different shapes the Moon appears to take as it travels around Earth. (p. C73)

photosynthesis (fō′tə sin′thə sis) A process in plants that uses energy from sunlight to make food from water and carbon dioxide. (p. A74)

phylum (fī′ləm), *pl.* **phyla** (fī′lə) A large group within a kingdom. Members share at least one major characteristic, like having a backbone. (p. A22)

physical change (fiz′i kəl chānj) A change that begins and ends with the same type of matter. *See* **chemical change.** (p. E44)

pistil (pis′təl) The part of the plant that produces the female sex cells, the eggs. (p. A84)

pitch (pich) The highness or lowness of a sound as determined by its frequency. (p. F59)

planet (plan′it) A satellite of the Sun. (p. C81)

pole (pōl) One of two ends of a magnet; where a magnet's pull is strongest. (p. F90)

pollen (pol′ən) Powdery grains in a flower that contain its male sex cells. (p. A84)

pollination (pol′ə nā′shən) The transfer of a flower's pollen from anther to pistil. (p. A84)

pollution (pə lü′shən) The adding of harmful substances to the water, air, or land. (p. A58)

population (pop′yə lā′shən) One type of organism living in an area. (p. A40)

pore space (pôr spās) The space between soil particles. (pp. C48, D38)

potential energy (pə ten′shəl en′ər jē) Energy that is stored or waiting to be used, giving an object the future ability to do work. (p. F14)

precipitation (pri sip′i tā′shən) Water in the atmosphere that falls to Earth as rain, snow, hail, or sleet. (p. D18)

predict (pri dikt′) To state possible results of an event or experiment. (p. S7)

prism (pri′zəm) An object that separates white light into the colors that make it up. (p. F42)

producer (prə dü′sər) An organism, such as a plant, that makes food. (p. A46)

protist (prō′tist) Any of the one-celled organisms that live in water. Some are plantlike and make their own food. Some are animal-like and are capable of motion. (p. A12)

pulley (pủl′ē) A machine made up of a rope, belt, or chain wrapped around a wheel with a groove in it. (p. F24)

pupa (pū′pə) A stage of some organisms that follows the larva stage; many changes take place as adult tissues and organs form. (p. B56)

R

radiation (rā′dē ā′shən) The transfer of energy through space. (p. F36)

reflection (ri flek′ shən) The bouncing of light waves off a surface. (p. F45)

reflex (rē′fleks′) The simplest inherited behavior that is automatic, like an animal scratching an itch. (p. B70)

refraction (ri frak′shən) The bending of light as it passes from one transparent material into another. (p. F46)

regeneration (rē jen′ə rā′shən) A form of reproduction in simple animals in which a whole animal develops from just a part of the original animal. (p. B60)

PRONUNCIATION KEY

a at; ā ape; ä far; âr care; ô law; e end; ē me; i it; ī ice; îr pierce; o hot; ō old; ôr fork; oi oil; ou out; u up; ū use; ü rule; ủ pull; ûr turn; hw white; ng song; th thin; <u>th</u> this; zh measure; ə about, taken, pencil, lemon, circus

relative age (rel′ə tiv āj) The age of something compared to the age of another thing. (p. C11)

reproduction (rē′prə duk′shən) The making of offspring. (p. B60)

reptile (rep′təl′) A cold-blooded vertebrate that lives on land and has a backbone, an endoskeleton, and waterproof skin with scales or plates. (p. B32)

resistor (ri zis′tər) A material through which electricity has difficulty flowing. (p. F80)

respiration (res′pə rā′shən) The using and releasing of energy in a cell. (p. A74)

respiratory system (res′pər ə tôr′ē sis′təm) The organ system that brings oxygen to body cells and removes waste gas. (p. B47)

retina (ret′ə nə) A tissue covering the back of the eye where light images are changed into signals that travel along the optic nerve to the brain. (p. F48)

revolve (ri volv′) To move in a circular or nearly circular path around something else. (p. C68)

rock cycle (rok sī′kəl) A never-ending process by which rocks are changed from one type to another. (p. C13)

root (rüt) The part of a tree that takes in water and other materials a plant needs to make food. (p. A70)

root hair (rüt hâr) One of the threadlike cells on a root that take in water and minerals from the soil. (p. A71)

rotate (rō′tāt) To spin around. (p. C66)

runoff (run′ôf′) The water that flows over Earth's surface but does not evaporate or soak into the ground. (p. D39)

S

scale (skāl) An instrument used to measure weight. (p. E19)

screw (skrü) An inclined plane twisted into a spiral. (p. F27)

sediment (sed′ə ment) Deposited rock particles and other materials that settle in a liquid. (p. C10)

sedimentary rock (sed′ə men′tə rē rok) Rock formed from bits or layers of rocks cemented together. (p. C10)

seed (sēd) An undeveloped plant with stored food sealed in a protective covering. (p. A82)

seismic wave (sīz′mik wāv) A vibration caused by rocks moving and breaking along faults. (p. C56)

seismograph (sīz′mə graf′) An instrument that detects, measures, and records the energy of earthquake vibations. (p. C54)

septic tank (sep′tik tangk) An underground tank in which sewage is broken down by bacteria. (p. D53)

series circuit (sîr′ēz sûr′kit) A circuit in which the objects are connected in a single path. (p. F82)

sewage (sü′ij) Water mixed with waste. (p. D53)

sewer (sü′ər) A large pipe or channel that carries sewage to a sewage treatment plant. (p. D53)

short circuit (shôrt sûr′kit) A situation that allows too much current to flow through a conductor. (p. F80)

simple machine (sim′pəl mə shēn′) A machine with few moving parts, making it easier to do work. The six types of simple machines are the lever, pulley, wheel and axle, inclined plane, wedge, and screw. (p. F20)

skeletal system (skel′i təl sis′təm) The organ system made up of bones. (p. B52)

soil profile (soil prō′fīl) A vertical section of soil from the surface down to bedrock. The more horizons in a soil profile the greater the relative age of the soil. (p. C45)

soil water (soil wô′tər) Water that soaks into the ground. (p. D10)

solar system (sō′lər sis′təm) The Sun and all the objects that orbit around it. (p. C81)

solid (sol′id) A state of matter that has a definite shape and takes up a definite amount of space. (p. E8)

sound wave (sound wāv) An area of bunched-up and spread-out air particles that moves outward in all directions from a vibrating object. (p. F55)

species (spē′shēz′) The smallest group into which an organism is classified. (p. A25)

spectrum (spek′trəm) A range of light waves with different wavelengths. (p. F42)

speed (spēd) The distance traveled in a certain amount of time (p. F8)

sperm (spûrm) The male sex cell. (p. B61)

sponge (spunj) The simplest kind of invertebrate. (pp. B8, B17)

spore (spôr) The cells in a seedless plant that grows into new organisms. (p. A88)

PRONUNCIATION KEY

a at; ā ape; ä far; âr care; ô law; e end; ē me; i it; ī ice; îr pierce; o hot; ō old; ôr fork; oi oil; ou out; u up; ū use; ü rule; ů pull; ûr turn; hw white; ng song; th thin; <u>th</u> this; zh measure; ə about, taken, pencil, lemon, circus

standard unit (stan'dərd ū'nit) A unit of measure that people agree to use. Units in the English system, such as the inch, pound, yard, and gallon are used mostly in the United States. *See* **metric system.** (p. E16)

star (stär) A hot sphere of gases that gives off energy. (p. C80)

state (stāt) Any of the three forms of matter—solid, liquid, or gas—that exist on Earth. (p. E8)

static electricity (stat'ik i lek tris'i tē) The buildup of an electric charge on a material. (p. F71)

stationary front (stā'shə ner ē frunt) An unmoving front where a cold air mass and a warm air mass meet. (p. D81)

stem (stem) The part of a tree that carries food, water and other materials to and from the roots and leaves. (p. A70)

stomata (stō'mə tə) *pl. n., sing.* **stoma** Pores in the bottom of leaves that open and close to let in air or give off water vapor. (p. A73)

stratus cloud (strā'təs kloud) A cloud that forms in a blanket-like layer. (p. D71)

streak plate (strēk plāt) A glass plate that a mineral can be rubbed against to find out the color of the streak it leaves. (p. C7)

subsoil (sub'soil') A hard layer of clay and minerals that lies beneath topsoil. (p. C45)

surface current (sûr'fis kûr'ənt) The movement of the ocean caused by steady winds blowing over the ocean. (p. D29)

switch (swich) A device that can open or close an electric circuit. (p. F79)

symmetry (sim'ə trē) The way an animal's body parts match up around a point or central line. (p. B8)

T

taproot (tap'rüt') A single, thick root that is one of the two main types of plant roots. *See* **fibrous root.** (p. A71)

temperature (tem'pər ə cher) A measure of how hot or cold something is. (p. F35)

terminus (tûr'mə nəs) The end, or outer margin, of a glacier where rock debris accumulates. (p. C35)

thermometer (thər mom'ə tər) An instrument used to measure temperature. (p. F35)

tide (tīd) The rise and fall of ocean water levels. (p. D30)

tissue (tish'ü) A group of similar cells that work together to carry out a job. (p. A14)

topsoil (top'soil') The dark, top layer of soil, rich in humus and minerals, in which many tiny organisms live and most plants grow. (p. C45)

trait (trāt) A characteristic of a living thing. (p. A21)

translucent (trans lü′sənt) Letting only some light through, so that objects on the other side appear blurry. (p. F49)

transparent (trans pâr′ənt) Letting all light through, so that objects on the other side can be seen clearly. (p. F49)

transpiration (tran′spə rā′shən) A plant's release of excess water vapor through the stomata on the underside of its leaves. (pp. A73, D41)

trough (trôf) The lowest part of a wave. (p. D32)

use numbers (ūz num′bərz) To order, count, add, subtract, multiply, and divide to explain data. (p. S7)

use variables (ūz vâr′ē ə bəlz) To identify and separate things in an experiment that can be changed or controlled. (p. S7)

vacuole (vak′ū ōl′) The cell's holding bin for food, water, and wastes. (p. A9)

vein (vān) One of the bundle of tubes in a stem that carry water to the leaf and take food from the leaf to the stem and roots. (p. A73)

vertebrate (vûr′tə brāt′) An animal with a backbone. (p. B8)

vibration (vī brā′shən) The back-and-forth motion of an object. (p. F54)

virus (vī′rəs) Nonliving particles smaller than cells that are able to reproduce only inside living cells. (p. A16)

visible spectrum (viz′ə bəl spek′trəm) The seven colors of light that make up white light: red, orange, yellow, green, blue, indigo, violet. (p. F42)

volt (vōlt) A unit for measuring the force with which negative charges flow. (p. F96)

voltage (vōlt′tij′) A measure of the force with which negative charges flow. (p. F96)

volume (vol′ūm) The amount of space an object takes up. (p. E17)

PRONUNCIATION KEY

a at; ā ape; ä far; âr care; ô law; e end; ē me; i it; ī ice; îr pierce; o hot; ō old; ôr fork; oi oil; ou out; u up; ū use; ü rule; u̇ pull; ûr turn; hw white; ng song; th thin; <u>th</u> this; zh measure; ə about, taken, pencil, lemon, circus

warm front (wôrm frunt) A boundary between air masses where the warm air mass slides up and over the cold air mass. (p. D80)

warm-blooded (wôrm'blud'id) Said of an animal with a constant body temperature. (p. B28)

water conservation (wôtər kon'sər vā'shən) The use of water-saving methods. (p. D54)

water cycle (wô'tər sī'kəl) The continuous movement of water between Earth's surface and the air, changing from liquid to gas to liquid. (p. D20)

water table (wô'tər tā'bəl) The upper area of groundwater. (p. D39)

water treatment plant (wô'tər trēt'mənt plant) A place where water is made clean and pure. (p. D52)

water vapor (wô'tər vā'pər) A gas in Earth's atmosphere. (p. D6)

wave (wāv) An up-and-down movement of water. (p. D32)

wavelength (wāv'lengkth') The distance from the top of one wave to the top of the next. (pp. D32, F42)

wedge (wej) A moving inclined plane. (p. F27)

weight (wāt) The measure of the pull of gravity between an object and Earth. (pp. E19, F12)

wet cell (wet sel) A device that produces electricity using two different metal bars placed in an acid solution. (p. F81)

wheel and axle (hwēl and ak'səl) A simple machine made of a handle or axle attached to the center of a wheel. (p. F25)

work (wûrk) The use of a force to move an object a certain distance (p. F13)

Index

A

Acceleration, F8
Acid rain, A59
Adaptations, B66–67, B69*, B73
Adult stage, B56, B57
Age, relative, C11
Air, D63*, D64, D66–69, D78
Air masses, D78–81
Air pollution, A59
Air pressure, D67, D69, D70*, D72
Air temperature, D66, D72
Al–Battani, C90–91
Algae, A12
Alligators, B32
Alloys, E38
Alternating current (AC), F94
Altitude, climate and, D87
Alvarez, Luis, A24
Alvarez, Walter, A24
Amber, C20
Ammeter, F78–79
Amoeba, A12
Amperes, F78–79
Amphibians, B28, B31, B45*, B47
Amplifier, F60
Amplitude, F59
Anemometer, D72
Animals, B4–41
    cells in, A7–11
    characteristics of, B5*–6
    development of, B54–59
    differences among, B8–10
    endangered, A36–37, B12–13
    energy sources for, B7
    helping people, B36, B71
    life cycle of, B58
    life span of, B59
    modeling cells of, A11*
    organ systems of, B44–53
    petrified, C21
    relationship to plants, A90–91
    reproduction in, B60–62
    soil formation and, C44
    survival by, B64–75
    tool use among, F21
    water in, D12
    with backbones. See Vertebrates.
    without backbones. See Invertebrates.
Anther, A84
Ant plant, A78–79
Apollo missions, C71
Arachnids, B21
Area, E17
Armadillos, B72
Arthropods, B16, B21–23
Aryabhata the First, C90–91
Ascaris, B18
Asteroids, C86
Atmosphere, D6, D11, D16–17, D64, D65
Atoms, E32, F70–71
Ax, F20
Axis of Earth, C67
Axles, wheels and, F20, F25

B

Bacteria, A13, C44
Bacteriologists, A94–95
Balance, E8, E19
Baleen whale, A33
Bar magnets, F88, F89*–90
Barometer, D70*, D72
Basalt, C9, C13
Bats, A32, B51
Batteries, F81
Beaches, D9
Beavers, F21
Bedrock, C44, C45
Berzelius, Jöns Jacob, E40–41
Bicycles, F28, F29
Bilateral symmetry, B9
Birds, B28, B33, B48, B49
Blackout, F76
Bladder, B47
Blind salamander, A33
Blood, B46
Body color, B65*–66, B67
Body plans, symmetrical, B8–10
Bones, A32, A33, C21
Bony fish, B28, B29, B30
Bottom dwellers, B30
Brains, comparison of, B50
Bryce Canyon, Utah, C4
Budding, B60
Buoyancy, E7
Butterflies, B9, B68

C

Cactus, A76
Calcite, C7, C8
California condor, B13
Camels, D4
Camouflage, B66
Canis familiaris, A25
Carbon, C21
Carbon dioxide, A70, A73, A74, D24, D25, D41, D64, D78
Carnivores, A48
Carrots, A71
Cartilaginous fish, B28, B29, B30
Cast (fossil), C19*
Caterpillars, A68, B6
Cell membrane, A9
Cells, A4–11, A14, A17
    chemical changes in, E56
    classifying organisms and, A20, A21
    definition of, A7
    in plant stem, A72
    jobs of, A10
    life span and division of, B59
    modeling, A11*
    of onion plant, A55*
    plant vs. animal, A7–11
    sex, A85, A87, A88
    shapes of, A10

*Indicates an activity related to this topic.

Cells, electric, F81
Cell wall, A8
Celsius scale, F35
Centipedes, B21, B22
CFCs, D74–75
Charge, electrical, F70–71
Cheetah, B34
Chemical changes in matter,
    E50–57, E51*
    causes of, E53
    characteristics of, E52–53
    in the real world, E56
    preventing, E55*
    products of, E54
Chemical energy, F15, F16
Chemists, E62–63
Chesapeake Bay cleanup, A60
Chitin, B21
Chlorine, D52
Chlorine gas, E53
Chlorophyll, A7, A73, A74
Chloroplasts, A8, A47
Chromosomes, A9
Cichlid, B30
Circuit breakers, F84
Circuits, F78–79
    kinds of, F82–83
    protection of, F84
    sizes of, F86–87
Circulatory system, B45*, B46
Cirrus clouds, D71
Classes, A22–23
Classification
    of matter, E31*–39
    of organisms, A18–35, A19*,
        B26, B28–35*
    skills in, A18, A24*, B14,
        B26, E30
Clean Air Act, A60
Clean Water Act, A60
Climate, D84–89
Clones, B60
Closed circuit, F78–79
Cloud cover, D71
Clouds, D17, D20, D21, D71,
    E56
Clovis point, F20
Cnidarians, B16, B17, B46
Coastlines, D34
Coconuts, A80

Cold–blooded animals, B28
Cold fronts, D81, D83
Comets, C86, C87*
Communication skills, D46, E42,
    F88
Community, A40, A41
Compass, F8
Compound machines, F29
Compounds, E36–37, E54
Computer chips, F86–87
Concave lens, F47
Condensation, D17, D19, D20,
    D21
Conduction, F36
Conductors, F34–35, F72, F80*
Conglomerate, C10
Constellations, C88
Consumers, A46, A47, A48
Continental shelf, D7
Continental slope, D7
Contraction, F37
Convection, F36
Convex lens, F46
Copernicus, Nicolaus,
    C90–91
Copper acetate, E52
Copying behavior, B71
Coral reefs, B24
Cornea, F48
Crabs, B48
Craters, C71
Creep meter, C59
Crescent Moon, C72, C73
Crest of wave, D32, D33
Crocodiles, B32
Crustaceans, B21, B22
Crust of Earth, C58
Crystals, D22
Cumulus clouds, D71
Current electricity, F76–87
    circuits, F78–79, F82–84,
        F86–87
    delivery to homes, F96
    flow of, F80
    light bulbs, F77*–78
    safe use of, F98
    sources of, F81
    static electricity vs., F78*
Currents, ocean, D28–29
Cytoplasm, A9

Dams, D43
Damselflies, B57
Dandelions, A71, A86
Decomposers, A46, A47, A48, A49*
Deep ocean current, D28
Density, E20*–21
Deposition, D34
Desalination, D56–57
Deserts, A38, A44, A54
Development, B54–59
Diamond, C7
Diaphragm, B47
Digestive system, A15, B48–49
Dingos, A57
Dinosaurs, C14, C18
Direct current (DC), F94
Discharge, electrical, F72, F73–74
Diseases, A56
Dodo bird, A34
Dogs, B36, B71
Dolphins, B34
Dormant trees, A76
Dormouse, B70
Droughts, A56, D42
Drumlin, C34, C35
Dry cell, F81
Dry ice, D24, D25
Duckbilled platypus, B34
Dust storms, C40
Dusty seaside sparrow, A34

E

Eardrum, F57
Earle, Dr. Sylvia, D94–95
Ears, F57
Earth, C30–61, C53*, C82, C83
    as frame of reference, F7
    as magnet, F91
    earthquakes, C54–57, C59
    forces shaping, C33–41, D11
    Moon compared to, C70–71
    movement of, C65*–66, C68
    rotation of, D29

*Indicates an activity related to this topic.

seasons of, C68–69
soil, A42, C42–51, D37*–39
structure of, C58
Earthquakes, C54–57, C55*, C59
Echinoderms, B16, B20
Ecology, A40
Ecosystems, A40–61
     changes in, A54–61, A55*
     differences between, A42–43
     food chains in, A48, A49, A50, B7
     food webs in, A50
     kinds of, A44–45
     resources needed by, A56
     roles of organisms in, A46–49
Eels, B30
Efficiency of machines, F30
Effort force, F22
Egg, B61
Egg stage, B56, B57
Electric meter, reading, F97*
Electric motor, F93
Electrical charge, F70–71
Electrical discharge, F72, F73–74
Electrical energy, F15, F16
Electricity. *See also* Current electricity; Static electricity.
     from magnets, F94–95
     produced by water, D50
Electrodes, F81
Electromagnetic spectrum, F42–43
Electromagnets, F92*–93
Electron microscope, A94–95
Elements, E32–36
El Niño, D87
Embryo, A33, A85, B61
Emerald tree boa, A26
Endangered animals, A36–37,
     B12–13
Endoplasmic reticulum, A8, A9
Endoskeleton, B20
Energy, F14–16
     forms of, A52–53, F14–16
     from lightning, F74
     light as, F42
English system of measurement,
     E16
Environment, A43, A47, C24, C71
Epidermis of leaves, A73
Equus, A30
Erosion, C13, C47
     by glaciers, C33–37

by other agents, C38, C40–41
by waves, D34
Erratics, C37
Esophagus, B49
Estuary, D9
Euglena, A12, A14
Evaporation
     heat energy and, E48*
     separating mixtures by, E35
     surface area and, D44*
     of water, D15*–17, D18*, D19,
          D20, D21, D44*
Evergreen, A76
Evolution, A30
Excretory system, B47
Exoskeleton, B21
Expand, Expansion, F37
Experience, learning from, B71
Experimentation skills, C32, D14,
     D26, D76, E14, E48*, E50, F40,
     F52
Extinct, Extinctions, A33, A34,
     C14
Exxon Valdez, A58
Eyes, B51*, F48–49

Fabrics, from plastics, E12
Fahrenheit scale, F35
Family, A22–23
Faraday, Michael, F99
Farming, water used in, D50
Fat, for warmth, F33*
Fault, C56
Feldspar, C6, C8
Ferris wheel, F25
Fertilization, A85, B61
Fertilizers, C47, D51
Fibrous roots, A71
Filters, E35
Filtration, D52
Finches, F21
Fins, B30, B67
Fire, ecosystem and, A57
First–class lever, F23
First Quarter Moon, C73
Fish, B28, B29–30, B44, B45*, B46,
     B51

Fixed pulley, F24
Flamingo, B33
Flatworms, B16, B18
Floods, D43
Flowering plants, A87
Fluorite, C7
Focus of earthquake, C56
Food, animal digestion of, B48
Food chains, A48, A49, A50, B7
Food web, A50, B7
Footprint, calculating animal size
     from, C23
Forces, F7–13
     effort, F22
     friction, F8, F11, F30
     gravity as, F12
     motion and, F7–13
     work and, F13
Forests, A26, A42–43, A45, A57
Fossil fuels, F38
Fossils, A30–31*, C14, C16–27
     formation of, C18–21
     learning from, C17*–18, C24
     processing, C22
     types of, C18–19
Frame of reference, F6–7
Freeze, D19
Frequency of sound wave, F58
Freshwater lakes and rivers, A45
Friction, F8, F11, F30
Frogs, B44, B48, B49, B50
Fronts, D80–81, D82
Fulcrum, F22
Full Moon, C72
Fungi, A13, C44
Fur, B67
Furrows, D50
Fuse, F84

Galena, C7, C8
Galileo, C76, C90–91
Gamma rays, F42–43
Gamma waves, F42–43
Garbage, managing, E11
Garbologists, E24–25
Gas, E9, E47
Gears, F28

Generators, F94–95
Genus, A22–23, A25
Geologists, C6
Geranium, A70
Germination, A82
Gibbous Moon, C72, C73
Gill flaps, B30
Gills, B29, B67
Giraffe, B67
Gizzard, B49
Glacial till, C35
Glaciers, C33*–37, D11
Glass, volcanic, C9
Global winds, D87
Gneiss, C12
Gobi Desert, C26
Goliath Bird Eater, B38–39
Grain beetle, B56
Grams, E8
Grand Canyon, C54
Granite, C6, C9
Grasshopper, B52
Grasslands, A44, A54
Gravity, C38, C70, D30, E19, F12
Gravity meter, C59
Great Barrier Reef, B24
Great Dark Spot, C85
Great Lakes, D83
Great Red Spot, C84
Greenhouse effect, D88
Green sea turtle, A37
Grid, electric, F86
Grounded, F74
Groundwater, D10, D11, D38, D40, D48, E24–25
Groups in periodic table, E33
Gulf, D9
Gypsy moths, A68

Habitat, A40, A41
Hail, D18, D22
Hailstones, D22
Half Moon, C73
Halley's comet, C87
Hawk, B33
Hearing aid, F60
Hearing, tools for, F60

Heart, B45*, B46
Heat, D21, F32–39
Heat energy, D16, D19, E47, E48*
Helping Hands program, B71
Henry, Joseph, F93, F99
Herbivores, A48
Heredity, B62*
Hibernation, B70
High Plains Climate Zone, D84–85
History of Science
    Berzelius, E40–41
    Views of the Universe, C90-91
Honeybees, B74–75
Hookworm, B18
Horizon, soil, C45
Hornblende, C6, C8
Horn tooth, B29
Horse, B34
Hot–air balloon, F62–63
Houston, Dr. Cliff, A94–95
Hubble Telescope, C77
Humans
    arms of, A32
    brain of, B50
    digestive system of, A15
    life cycle of, B58
    role in extinctions, A34
Humidity, D66, D72
Humpback whale flipper, A32
Humus, C44
Hurricanes, D34, D90–91
Hydra, B17, B60
Hydroelectric power plants, D50
Hydrogen, C80
Hygrometer, D72
Hypatia, C90–91
Hypothesis, forming, B69*
Hyracotherium, A30

Ice ages, C37
Icebergs, D8
Ice caps, D8, D11
Ice particles, D20
Igneous rocks, C9
Imprints, C18
Inclined plane, F20, F26, F27

Incoming angle, F45
Incoming rays, F45
Industry, water used in, D50
Inertia, F11
Inference–making skills, B4, B54, C4, C64, D4, D36, D62, D70*, E4, F32
Infrared light, F42–43
Inherited behavior, B70
Inner core of Earth, C58
Inner ear, F57
Inner planets, C82–83
Insects, B21, B23
    eyes of, B51
    incomplete metamorphosis in, B57
    pollination by, A84
Instinct, B70
Insulators, F34, F72
Interglacial periods, C37
International Space Station, F102–103
Interpreting data, C74
Interpretive skills, C16, C74
Invertebrates, B8, B14–25, B47
    budding in, B60
    characteristics of, B15*–16
    classifying, B16–23*, B24
    digestive system of, B49
    muscular system of, B52
Irrigation, D50

Jackson, Dionne, E62–63
Jawless fish, B28, B29
Jellyfish, B17
Joints, B52
Jones, Brian, F62
Jupiter, C84, C85

Kangaroos, A57
Kepler, Johannes, C90–91

*Indicates an activity related to this topic.

Kidneys, B47
Kilograms, E8
Kinetic energy, F14, F16
Kingdoms, A20–21, A22–23
Kittens, B54
Knife, F20, F27

L

Lakes, A45, D8, D11
Lampreys, B29
Landfills, E24–25
Land pollution, A59
Larva stage, B56
Lasers, F15, F50
Last Quarter Moon, C73
Lateral moraine, C34
Latitude, climate and, D86
Lava, C9, C13
Law of reflection, F45
Leaf cells, A10
Learning, B71
Leaves, A15, A24*, A69*, A70, A73, A83
Leeches, B19
"Leftover" structures of organisms, A33
Legs, B67
Length, E16
Lenses, F47
Levers, F22–23*
Life cycle, A87, B58, B63
Life functions, A6–7
Life span, B59
Light, F40–51
    absorbing, F49*
    characteristics of, F42–43
    eyes and, F48–49
    lasers, F15, F50
    mixing colors of, F41*
    motion of, F44
    reflection, F45
    refraction, F46–47
Light energy, F15
Lightning, F73–74
Lightning rods, F74
Light pipes, F50
Limb bones, A32

Limestone, C10, C12, C14
Linnaeus, Carolus, A25
Liquids, E9, E17, E46
Liquid wastes, B47
Liters (L), E17
Littering, A59, A60
Liver, B49
Living things, A6–7. *See also* Animals; Plants; Organisms.
    interaction with nonliving things, A39*–40
    water in, D12
Lizards, B32, B48
Load, F22
Lobsters, B22, B48
Luster, C7

M

Machines, F20–31
    compound, F29
    efficiency of, F30
    simple. *See* Simple machines.
Magma, C9, C13
Magnetic field, F91
Magnetite, C8, F90
Magnets, F88–99
    bar, F88, F89*–90
    Earth as, F91
    electricity from, F94–95
    electromagnets, F92*–93
    properties of, F90
Magnifying glass, F47
Mammals, B28, B34–35
    fat in, F33*
    heart of, B46
Mammoths, A34, A62–63, C20
Manatees, B12
Mantle of Earth, C58
Maps, weather, D82–83
Marble, C12
Marshmallows, E56
Marianas Trench, D7
Marine sanctuaries, D94–95
Mars, C78, C82, C83
Marshes, D8
Mass, E8, E10
Mass extinctions, A24

Matter, E4–63
    changes in, E42–57, E43*, E51*
    characteristics of, E8–10*
    classifying, E31*–39, E36*
    definition of, E6
    identifying, E5*
    measuring, E14–26, E15*, E18*, E20*
    properties of, E6–7, E10
    states of, E8–9, E10, E45–47
Mealworms, B55*–56
Measuring skills, F9*
Mechanical energy, F15
Meet People in Science
    Earle, Dr. Sylvia, D94–95
    Houston, Cliff, A94–95
    Jackson, Dionne, E62–63
    Ochoa, Dr. Ellen, F102–103
    Patterson, Dr. Coretta, B78–79
    Sanchez, Dr. Pedro, C94–95
Melting, D19, D21
Mendeleyev, Dmitry, E33
Mercury, C82, C83
Merychippus, A30
Mesohippus, A30
Mesosphere, D65
Metamorphic rocks, C12–13
Metamorphosis, B56–57
Meteor Crater, C86
Meteorite, A24, C87
Meteorologists, D94–95
Meteors, C86
Methane, E24–25
Metric system, E16, E22
Mica, C6, C8
Microorganisms, A12–13
Microscope, electron, A94–95
Microwaves, F42–43
Middle ear, F57
Mid–ocean ridge, D7
Midwest/Ohio Valley Climate Zone, D84–85
Migrating instinct, B70
Mild forest lands, A44
Milliliters (mL), E17
Millipedes, B21, B22
Mimicry, B68
Mina, E22
Minerals, C6–8*, C47
Mitochondria, A8, A9
Mixtures, E34–36*, E38

Modeling skills, A11, C78
Molds (fossils), C18–C19*
Molds (organism), A49
Moles, F21
Mollusks, B16, B20
Molting, B21
Monarch butterflies, B68
Monkeys, Helping Hands, B71
Moon, the, C70–74
   movement of, C65*–66
   tides and, D30, D31
Moons, C83, C84, C85
Moraine, C34, C35
Moss plant, A88
Moths, B6, B66, B67
Motion, F4–13, F5*, F19*
   forces and, F7–13
   of light, F44
   position and, F6
   speed, F8
Motors, electric, F93
Mountains, D7, D86
Mouth, B49
Movable pulley, F24
Mummies, C20
Muscle tissue, A14
Muscular system, B52
Mushroom, A13

N

National Geographic Society
   Amazing Stories
     circling the globe in hot–air
      balloon, F62–63
     desalination, D56–57
     fossils, C26–27
     spider giants, B38–39
     woolly mammoth, A62–63
Neck, B67
Nectar, A84
Neptune, C84, C85
Nerve cells, A10
Nervous system, B50
Neutron star, E21
New England Climate Zone,
   D84–85
New Moon, C72, C73

Newt, B31
Newton, Sir Isaac, F10
Newton (unit of weight), E19, F10
Nitrogen, D64, D78
Nonwoody stems, A72
North Pole, C69
Northwestern Climate Zone,
   D84–85
Nuclear energy, F15, F95
Nucleus, A9
Numbers, using, C23, F97*
Nymph stage, B57

O

Observation skills, A38, B10, B44,
   C42, F18
Obsidian, C9
Ocean birds, D9
Oceanographers, D94–95
Oceans, D6, D7, D20, D27–35
   coastlines changed by, D34
   movement of, C38, D27*–34,
     D32*
Ochoa, Dr. Ellen, F102–103
Octopus, B14, B48
Oil spill, A58
Omnivores, A48
Onion plant, A55*
Opaque, F49
Open circuit, F78–79
Open sea ecosystems, A45
Orbit, C68
Orders, A22–23
Organisms, A6–7. See also Animals.
   classification of, A18–35, A19*,
     A24*, A31*
   roles in ecosystems, A46–49
Organs, A15
Organ systems, A15, B44–53
   circulatory system, B45*, B46
   digestive system, A15, B48–49
   excretory system, B47
   muscular system, B52
   nervous system, B50
   respiratory system, B47
   skeletal system, B52
   special sense organs, B51
Ostrich, B33

Outer core of Earth, C58
Outer ear, F57
Outer planets, C84–85
Outgoing angle, F45
Outgoing rays, F45
Outwash plains, C37
Ovary, in plants, A85
Overpopulation, A57
Oxygen, A6, B47, D64, D78
Ozone layer, D74–75

P

Pangolins, B72
Panthera, A25
Parallel circuit, F82
Parasites, B18
Patterson, Dr. Coretta, B78–79
Penguin, B33
People. See Humans; Meet People
   in Science.
Peppered moths, B66, B67
Performance Assessment
   energy, F104
Periodic table, E32–33
Permeability of soil, C49
Pesticides, D51
Pet Partners, B36
Petrified, C21
Pharmacists, E62–63
Phases of the Moon, C73
Phloem cells, A72
Photosynthesis, A74, A75*
Phylum, A22–23, B16
Physical adaptations, B67
Physical changes in matter,
   E42–49, E43*
   in position or texture, E45
   in size or shape, E44, E45
   in state, E45–48*
   in the real world, E56
Piccard, Bertrand, F62
Pistil, A84
Pitch, F59
Pith cells, A72
Planarian, B15, B18, B60
Plane, inclined, F20, F26, F27
Planets, C81–85
   inner, C82–83

*Indicates an activity related to this topic.

outer, C84–85
Plants, A68–89
    cactus vs. evergreen, A76
    cells in, A7–11, A14
    dormant, A76
    incredible, A78–79
    leaves of, A15, A24*, A69*,
        A70, A73, A83
    life cycle of flowering plants, A87
    modeling cells of, A11*
    organs of, A15
    petrified, C21
    photosynthesis in, A74, A75*
    relationship to animals, A90–91
    respiration in, A74, A75*
    roots of, A70, A71, A83
    seeds of, A82–86, A91
    stems of, A70, A72, A83
    sunlight and, A41*
    water in, D12, D41
    with spores, A88
Plastics, recycled, E12
Pluto, C84, C85
Poles, magnetic, F90
Pollen, A84, A90–91
Pollen tube, A85
Pollination, A84, A90–91
Pollution, A58, A60, E56
    from fossil fuels, F38
    from landfills, E24–25
    of water, A58, A60, D51
Polyps, B24
Popcorn, E56
Populations, A40, A41
Porcupine, B72
Pore spaces, C48–49, D38, D43
Position, E45, F6
Potential energy, F14
Pouches, mammals with, B35
Pound, E22
Precipitation, D18–19, D21, D22, D24
    runoff from, D39*, D43
Predator fish, B30
Predicting skills, A75*, B64, C52, F76
Pressure, D67, D69, D70*, D72
Primary waves, C57
Prisms, F42–43
Process skills
    classifying, A18, A24*, B14,
        B26, E30

communicating, D46, E42, F88
experimenting, C32, D14, D26,
    D76, E14, E48*, E50, F40, F52
glacier flow, C36*
hypothesizing, B69*
inferring, B4, B54, C4, C64, D4,
    D36, D62, D70*, E4, F32
interpreting, C16, C74
measuring, F9*
modeling, A11, C78
observing, A38, B10, B44, C42,
    F18
predicting, A75*, B64, C52, F7
using numbers, C23, F97*
using variables, A80, D44*,
    D62, F4
Producers, A46, A47, A48
Project Lokahi, A36–37
Properties, E6
Protective resemblance, B66
Protists, A12
Ptolemy, C90–91
Puffer fish, B72
Pulleys, F19*, F20, F24
Pupa stage, B56
Pupil, F48
Pyrite, C7, C8

Quartz, C6, C8
Quills, B72

Radial symmetry, B9
Radiation, F36
Radio waves, F42–43
Rain, D18, D22, D72, D77*
Rain forests, A26, A45, A57
Rain gauge, D72
Rainmaking, D24–25
Ramp, F26
Rays (animal), B30
Rays (light), D74–75, F44–45

Receiver, F60
Rectangle, area of, E17
Recycling, E11, E12
Red blood cell, A10
Red–breasted toucan, A26
Red–eyed green tree frog, A26
Red giant, E21
Reef fish, B30
Reflection, F45
Reflex, B70
Refraction, F46–47
Regeneration, B60
Relative age, C11
Reproduction, B60–62
Reptiles, B28, B32
Resemblance, protective, B66
Resistors, F80
Respiration, A74, A75*
Respiratory system, B47
Retina, F48
Revolution of Earth, C68
Rivers, A45, A40, D8, D11, D20
Robotics, F102–103
Rock cycle, C13
Rock debris, C34–35
Rock layers, A31
Rocks, C4–15
    breakup of, C44
    igneous, C9
    interpreting, C5*–8
    layers, C14
    metamorphic, C12–13
    minerals, C6–8*, C47
    sedimentary, C10–11, C18
    water flow through, D37*–38
Rock salt, C10
Root hairs, A71
Roots of plants, A70, A71, A83
Rotation of Earth, C66, C67, D29
Roundworms, B16, B18
Runoff, D39*, D43
Rust, E37

Salamander, B31
Salt, E37
Saltwater communities, D9

Saltwater shores, A45

Sanchez, Dr. Pedro, C94–95

Sandstone, C10

Sandworms, B19

Satellites of the Sun, C81

Saturn, C84, C85

Scale, E19

Schaefer, Vincent, D24

Science Magazine

    alternative forms of energy,
      A52–53

    circuits, F86–87

    dancing bees, B74–75

    endangered animals, A36–37,
      B12–13

    erosion, C40–41

    ozone layer, D74–75

    plant–animal relationship,
      A90–91

    plants around the world,
      A78–79

    rainmaking, D24–25

    telescopes, C76–77

    views of the universe, C90–91

    wild weather, D90–91

Scissors, F29

Scolopendra, B22

Scorpions, B21

Screwdriver, F25

Screws, F20, F27

Sea anemones, B17, D9

Seas, D6

Seasons, C68–69

Sea star, B9, B20, B48

Secondary waves, C57

Second–class lever, F23

Sedimentary rocks, C10–11, C18

Sediments, C10, C11*

Seed coat, A82, A83

Seedling, A82, A83

Seeds, A81–86, A91

    dispersal of, A86

    formation of, A84–85

    growth of, A81*, A82–84

    parts of, A83

Segmented worms, B16, B19, B49

Seismic waves, C56–57

Seismogram, C57

Seismographs, C54, C57

Sense organs, special, B51

Septic tank, D53

Series circuit, F82

Sewage, D53

Sewers, D53

Sex cells, A85, A87, A88

Shadows, F44

Shale, C10

Shape, volume and, E18*

Shark brain, B50

Sharks, B30

Shekel, E22

Shell, B67

Shore, D7

Short circuit, F80, F84

Silver iodide, D25

Simple machines, F20–28

    gears, F28

    inclined plane, F20, F26, F27

    levers, F22–23*

    pulleys, F19*, F20, F24

    screws, F20, F27

    wedges, F20, F27

    wheels and axles, F20, F25

Size, heat and, F37

Skeletal system, B52

Skeletons, A29*–30

Skin, E56

Skin cells, A14

Skunks, B72

Sleet, D18, D22

Smog, A59

Snake, B32, B51

Snow, D18, D22

Sodium, E53

Soil, C42–51

    composition of, C43*–44

    effect on ecosystems, A42

    layering of, C45

    permeability of, C49

    runoff and, D39

    similarities and differences in,
      C46–49

    water flow through, C48*–49,
      D37*–38

Soil profile, C45

Soil water, D10, D11, D38

Solar system, C78–93, C79*

    asteroids, C86

    comets, C86, C87*

    meteors, C86

    moons, C83, C84, C85

    planets, C81–85

    sun, C80–81, F15

Solids, E8, E17, E46

Solid wastes, B49

Sound, F52–61

    differences among, F58–59

    ears and, F57

    tools for hearing, F60

    travel through different
      materials, F56

    vibrations and, F53*–55

Sound wave, F55, F58–59

Southeastern Climate Zone, D84–85

Southern Climate Zone, D84–85

Southwestern Climate Zone, D84–85

Sow bug, B72

Speakers, F60

Species, A22–23, A25

    endangered, A36–37

Spectrum, F42–43

Speed, F8

Sperm, B61

Spherical symmetry, B9

Spiders, B21, B38–39, B70

Spiny anteater, B34

Sponges, B8, B9, B16, B17, B46,
    B60

Spores, A88

Squid, B20, B48, B72

Standard units of measurement,
    E16–18*, E22–23

Stars, C80, C88, E21.
    See also Sun.

States of matter, E8–9, E10, E45–47

Static electricity, F68–74

    cause of, F70–71

    discharge of, F72

    from rubbed balloons, F69*

    lightning, F73–74

Stationary front, D81

Statue of Liberty, E50

Stem cells, A10

Stems of plants, A70, A72, A83

Stethoscope, F60

Stomach, B49

Stomata, A73

Stone plant, A78–79

Strain meter, C59

Stratosphere, D65

Stratus clouds, D71

Strawberry plant, A72

Streak plate, C7

Streams, D8, D11

Subsoil, C45

Sugar, A74, E37, E53, E54

*Indicates an activity related to this topic.